LAST OF THE BOOM SHIPS

**Oral Histories of the
U.S. Merchant Marine 1927-2000**

LAST OF THE BOOM SHIPS

Oral Histories of the U.S. Merchant Marine 1927-2000

By

Jim Whalen

ISBN: 1-58721-733-3

1stBook – rev. 6/5/00

About the Book

Fourteen men and one woman relate their experiences as Deck Officers on U.S. flag merchant ships - cargo ships in regular service, tramps, tankers, and the fastest passenger ship ever built, the *SS United States*. Carrying cargoes common as manhole covers, exotic as circus animals, dangerous as aviation gasoline, and dirty as coal, they sailed to travel poster ports like Rio de Janeiro, to war zones, and to ports like Mina al Ahmadi, Kuwait, where the 8 A.M. temperature is 120 degrees.

Share an old Master's remembrance of the thrill of sighting land for the first time, in 1927 from the fore topsail yard.

Cross the Atlantic in four days with the last Master of the *SS United States*, responsible for a 990-foot long ship, almost 2,000 passengers, and crew of over a thousand.

Suffer the horrors of war with a Second Mate on a tanker torpedoed by a German U-Boat, and a Deck Cadet, later Second Mate, on cargo ships under German air attacks in the Mediterranean and on the fearsome run to Murmansk, Russia.

Smell the oil on supertankers. Wear the dust on coal boats. Move alternative energy sources like natural gas from Sumatra and Borneo. Tramp for ore, grain, sugar, and fertilizer.

Spend days in port handling cargo on freighters with cargo booms or sixteen hours completely discharging and loading a containership. Pilot a 500-foot long ship in flooded Brazilian jungle river. Wait in mid-Atlantic for a tow after losing the ship's propeller. Nearly capsize fighting fire in the forward holds at dock in India, or try to extinguish a fire in the open Gulf of Mexico. Feel the collision as a Greek ore carrier tears open the port bow in Kobe, Japan.

Hold on as waves carry away lifeboats, while hove to in the eye of a hurricane, steering from the raised poop deck in drenching waves, or rolling thirty-five degrees with cargo containers stacked five high on deck.

Grieve over deaths from lack of oxygen in a tank. Rescue escaping Cubans and Vietnamese Boat People. Laugh at the returning Master who kissed his dog and then shook hands with his wife.

In their own words these officers matter-of-factly tell about doing their jobs - moving cargo and people safely and speedily all over the world

Dedicated to the memory of
Joe Strehle
navigator and bibliophile

PREFACE

I sailed as a Third Mate on U.S. flag merchant ships in the early-1960s. After getting married, I came ashore. When I resigned from American Export Lines, longtime hiring manager Tom Collins commented that women ruined more sailors than whiskey. For the following thirty-two years, I was a Special Agent of the Federal Bureau of Investigation and kept up with the maritime industry through my membership in the Alumni Association of the State University of New York Maritime College. Like people who never travel but always have a valid passport, I keep my Merchant Marine license current.

Some of the conversations at alumni meetings sounded like oral histories of America's Merchant Marine. The investigator in me recognized that, as our merchant fleet shrinks, this information needed to be recorded, or a valuable piece of Americana would be lost.

Fourteen men and one woman related their experiences as deck officers on U.S. flag merchant ships to me. As far back as 1927, they sailed on, or as one insisted, *in*, cargo ships in regular service, tramps, tankers, and the grand passenger liner *SS United States*. They carried cargoes as common as manhole covers, as exotic as live circus animals, as dangerous as aviation gasoline, and as dirty as coal to travel poster ports like Rio de Janiero, to war zones, and from oil ports like Mina al Ahmadi, Kuwait, where the 8 A.M. temperature was 120 degrees. Their voyages were mostly routine. Some were perilous, as in the cable, "Presently hove to in eye of hurricane. Will advise ETA later." These mariners are married, single, widowers, fathers, and a mother. Their hobbies include reading history, helping to restore a World War II Liberty ship, and collecting artifacts. Off the ships, they farm, work in allied or dissimilar industries, do volunteer work, play with their dogs, and, surprisingly, travel. They all try or tried to do the best job possible for their owners in moving general cargo, bulk cargoes like coal, oil or wheat, special cargoes like liquefied natural gas, or people all over the world safely and speedily, and sometimes under adverse conditions, for example, while fighting a fire aboard ship. They didn't see any glamour to it. They were just doing their jobs. To preserve this sense of duty, I've recorded their experiences in their own matter-of-fact and often understated words.

These officers are:

Captain Edward F. Carter, author of a work about his training on the barkentine *USS Newport*, Liberty ship Master in World War II, and a cargo surveyor in Baltimore, Maryland

Leroy J. Alexanderson, Commodore of United States Lines' fleet and Master of the fastest passenger ship ever built, the *SS United States*

Captain William Jay Atkinson, torpedoed in World War II and in 1960, Master of the *ST National Defender*, with the largest loaded displacement of any U.S. tanker, 82,678 tons

Captain Edward G. Fowler, forty-one years on ships and carrying military cargoes from World War II through the Vietnam War

Captain George E. white, going to sea in all kinds of vessels since 1935

Captain George E. McCarthy, son, grandson, and father of seafarers, who recorded every day he spent at sea in his log

Rear Admiral Richard A. Bauman, U.S. Coast Guard (Retired), a self-described "coal boat stiff"

John W. Ramsey, a Cook on Maine fishing boats at age eight, sailing as Second Mate on bulk carriers

Captain John W. Schindler, who recorded his twenty-three ships and 878,702 miles of blue water sailing in three pocketsize notebooks

Captain Douglas Glen, Master of a liquefied natural gas carrier

Captain Gerald V. Smeenk, who sailed with Lykes Brothers Steamship Company on the last of the boom ships

Captain John F. Wanner, a United States Lines Master when the company went bankrupt in 1986, stranding 140,000 containers of cargo in every corner of the world

Captain Arthur H. Sulzer, a deck officer, marine engineer, Naval Reservist, teacher, farmer, and businessman

Teresa Olsen Preston, a tanker Chief Mate working ashore

William G. Bullock, Jr., a Second Mate trying to become a Master

For my title I chose the simile of the passing of ships using cargo booms to chronicle the changes in the U.S. Merchant Marine. Booms on sailing ships were wooden spars that supported the sails. On traditional freighters they were long, steel poles supported at their base, or heel, in a joint called a gooseneck and at the head by topping lifts, guys, and falls. Cargo was attached to the falls for loading or discharge.

I offer my thanks to you who introduced me to deck officers. I limited my interviews to those whose voyages spanned a range of years, events, types of ships, cargoes, and trades. My own experiences as a mariner tell me that the book's topics are those typically of interest, be it to past, present, or future merchant mariners, weekend or arm-chair sailors, shoreside business people, scientists and engineers, economists, or historians.

Thanks also to my friends at The Writer's Center, Bethesda, Maryland: Frank Duncan, Bonnie Matheson, Melissa Pear, and Jerilynn Watson, for encouraging me to complete this book and to the center's Director, Al Lefcowitz, for his invaluable advice; and to my friend John Hodor for all his computer assistance

To my readers, in the words of one shipowner's letter of instructions to a Master, "I wish you a safe, speedy, and prosperous voyage."

Jim Whalen

WEIGHING ANCHOR

Most of these officers began their careers as deck cadets at maritime training schools - Maine Maritime Academy, Castine, Maine; the Massachusetts Nautical School, now the Massachusetts Maritime Academy, Buzzards Bay, Massachusetts; the Nautical School of the State of New York, New York City, now the State University of New York Maritime College, Fort Schuyler, The Bronx, New York; the defunct Pennsylvania State Nautical School, Philadelphia, Pennsylvania; or the U.S. Merchant Marine Academy, Kings Point, New York.

Captain Edward F. Carter's career afloat and ashore spanned six decades. At one point, he prepared a written account of his training, titling it *Tall Ship Tales; an Account of Two Years aboard the USS Newport, a Barkentine Rigged Training Ship of the New York State Nautical School, now the Maritime College of the State University of New York.*

Captain Carter:

I was born in Milwaukee, Wisconsin. After graduating from high school, I decided that I wanted to become a ship's captain. I started out for the New York Nautical School as a work-away, an unpaid crewman, on a Great Lakes freighter to Montreal in December 1927.

"The *USS Newport*, an auxiliary barkentine, was our training ship. She had been built by Bath Iron Works in 1897 as a gunboat ... square rigged foremast and schooner rigged main and mizzen .... She was of composite construction, steel frames, steel shell plating above the water line and wood planking below the water line. All decks were of wood. Her water line length was 168 feet, beam 36 feet, and she displaced a little over 1000 tons. Propulsion machinery was a triple expansion engine supplied by two coal-burning Scotch boilers.

1

Speed under power was about twelve knots. Sail area was about 12,000 square feet."

My first year, the *Newport* was docked at Bedloe's Island, the Statue of Liberty island, and the second year was at the Brooklyn Navy Yard. In the Deck Department we studied only nautical subjects. Each summer we took a three-month cruise.

There were four classes at the school at any one time, and the "Mugs," or Fourth Class Cadets, were subjected to hazing until it was outlawed.

"The hazing system as a whole was bad and occasionally got out of control. Sometimes the results required medical attention, but the "patient" usually complained of having slipped on the ice or fallen off a ladder."

After giving a very thorough report to an Upper Classman, I was dubbed "Nick Carter," after the fictional private eye, a nickname which has stayed with me.

My first training cruise went to Marseilles, Nice, Algiers, and Tangier.

"I had previously been away from home and at school for four years, but at no time did I feel so lonely as during my first night watch at sea. I was on lifebuoy watch at the very stern end of the quarterdeck. There was a fine drizzle, a cold wind, a heavy sea running ... my only companion was the taffrail log clicking off the miles farther and farther from home. The next morning we set foresail, fore topsail, fore topgallant, main topmast staysail and spanker. With a very lively ship we were making eleven knots."

"Our spar deck and gun deck were made of wood and, in addition to almost daily scrubdowns, were holystoned

2

occasionally. The holystone was a large and heavy block of sandstone fitted with a girth frame and long wooden handle. The deck was first wet down and sprinkled with sand ... the holystones were pulled back and forth ... removing surface dirt and also a very little bit of wood. The final result was a deck which could be called beautiful, but ... the holystones seemed to increase in weight with each stroke."

"Handling sails could be a pleasure, or it could be a nightmare, depending on temperature and weather ... always hard physical work because our canvas was heavy, nothing like yacht canvas. When wet and cold the canvas was stiff ... when reefing or furling, we just had to lean over the yard, make folds in the canvas, and grab it at the folds...."

"A sailing ship such as the *Newport* has about a hundred pieces of running rigging, ... pieces of rope which must be hauled in, slacked out or made fast, all in the ordinary routine of setting trimming and furling sails."

"In the dark a boy must be able to accurately locate every piece of running rigging on the ship. Failure to promptly identify a particular piece of gear called for several sound whacks across the bottom with that particular piece of rope."

"Bow lookout during the day was a good job ... perched on the fore topsail yard well removed from the work and hazing on deck. One of the most beautiful and welcome sights I have ever seen was the view of Cape St. Vincent, visible above the early morning mist on the twenty-third day out. What a thrill it was to sing out, "Land ho." "Where away?", came the question from below. "One point on the bow, Sir", I replied, forgetting for the moment all the unpleasantness and hazing."

"On leaving Las Palmas we took the steamship route intending to steam directly to New York ... On the fifth day out. Suddenly the ship vibrated from stem to stern, and then all was quiet. There could be only one explanation - the propeller had dropped off."

"We were placed on short rations as there was no telling when we would make port."

"We had a spell of radio problems."

"... eleven days after the loss of our propeller ... the U.S. Coast Guard Cutter *Chelan* arrived....took the messenger line ... to pull her Twelve-inch, manila towing hawser aboard....We then shackled the hawser to our starboard anchor chain and paid out about thirty fathoms of chain to give the hawser a bit more spring ...."

"It was a long tow - fifteen hundred miles - and the *Chelan* did it in nine days."

Tall Ship Tales

Our second summer cruise took us to London, Hamburg and Le Havre.

"...left Le Havre for Ponta Delgada, Azores. The second day out ... bucking heavy seas in the Bay of Biscay. The *Newport* was poking her nose into them, burying her bowsprit. This driving loosened the outer jib, and it had to be secured before it was ripped to shreds. I went along with three others to secure it, and, while were out there, the ship took a dive ... lifted our feet clear of the foot ropes on which we were standing. For a moment we were buried in water, upside down, and hanging on with hands only."

Tall Ship Tales

Of one hundred who started with me about fifteen graduated on November 21, 1929. I laughed at the morbid signatures on my diploma - Captain J.H. Tomb, Superintendent....and Dr. F.P. Graves, the Commissioner of Education for the State of New York.

Commodore Leroy J. Alexanderson:

I grew up in the Sheepshead Bay section of Brooklyn, New York, a son of Swedish immigrants, a fact I'm very proud of. I wanted to go to the U.S. Naval Academy, but was unable to get a Congressional appointment. A neighbor suggested that I apply to the New York Nautical School.

Three days after I reported aboard in 1928, the *USS Newport* left on its annual cruise. It was a rough experience. I returned home with cuts all over my hands and feet from climbing the rigging.

My class of 46 was down to about 23, when we graduated in June 1930."

Captain William Jay Atkinson:

I was born in Ellenberg Center, Clinton County, New York and grew up in Bloomingdale, New York. I had always wanted to go to sea. The advertisement for the New York Nautical School stated that the entire cost of the two-year course was approximately $130.00, and "Boys who are not rugged in physique and resolute in spirit, or boys who are afraid of manual work and the general privations of seafaring life, or the conditions of a military training, are not suited to become students at the School."

After graduation from high school in 1930, I took the entrance examination, but, since I was not very smart, didn't score high enough. I took it again and was admitted in 1931.

My training started just at the tail end of most sail training in the U.S., as a cadet aboard the *USS Newport*, a barkentine rigged gun boat of pre-Spanish American War vintage. She had a small, triple expansion, reciprocating steam engine powered by coal-fired boilers.

In the spring and summer of 1931, I made my first voyage, and the *Newport's* last, from New York to Bremerton, Washington, where the *Newport* was turned back to the Navy. That was my one and only voyage under sail and a most memorable experience. In exchange we received the *USS Procyon*, a Hog Island-type steam turbine freighter, renamed the *Empire State*.

Again because I wasn't very smart, I made an extra training cruise, thoroughly enjoying it. I graduated in October 1933, with a Third Mate's license.

Captain Edward G. Fowler:

I graduated from high school in my native Altoona, Pennsylvania in 1928, with no chance of continuing my education. My father and my sister worked for the Pennsylvania Railroad. I could have gone there, but that did not appeal to me. That summer, with some 400 others, I took an examination for Postal Clerk. My marks were fairly high, but ten points were added to the scores of the World War I veterans. I worked off and on and delivered mail at Christmas, but got no permanent job.

That winter, I got a circular letter from the Pennsylvania State Nautical School with pictures of cadets and the Schoolship *Annapolis*. Some 200 of us took a competitive examination in Philadelphia, and I passed. The closest I had ever come to an ocean was a visit with my uncle, a cook with the Merchants and Miners Steamship Company, aboard his ship in Baltimore.

The Schoolship *Annapolis*, a three-masted, schooner-rigged, sailing ship of 1010 deadweight tons with auxiliary steam power, was docked at the Philadelphia Navy Yard. Normally the ship made two cruises a year during the two-year course. When I was there, she was in drydock for a year, so I made only two cruises, to Northern Europe and the Caribbean. After the first six months of "boot days," I found out that I liked the time at sea and the ports that we visited.

I graduated in June 1931, with an AB's certificate and a Third Mate's license.

Captain George E. White:

I came by the sea naturally. My great-grandfather retired from the sea. My grandfather, David White, gave up the South China Sea trade when he began raising a family in Gloucester, Massachusetts and went on mackerel fishing smacks. His ice-laden vessel, returning from the Grand Banks with a catch, was never heard from again.

My father tried the sea in his early days, but became a professor at an Ivy League school. He continued his great admiration for the sea all his life. My family was not enthusiastic about my going to sea. When I continued, they said, "David is back."

The year 1935 was a low point in American shipping. A bloody strike in 1934 gave the maritime unions recognition. I got a probationary book with the International Seamen's Union on the East Coast, and the Shipping Board easily issued me an Ordinary Seaman certificate.

I shipped out with the Shepherd Line, a Boston company carrying general cargo to the West Coast of the U.S. and lumber back. I spent several months on a couple of intercoastal trips on the SS Sagebrush, a World War I Shipping Board ship. She was a real boom ship, with five-ton booms at each of her five hatches and "jumbo," heavy lift, gear at hatches number three and five. Times were rough. ABs were making $35.00 per month with the possibility of working up to $62.50.

Eventually, I joined the 30-man crew of the yacht Happy Days as an Ordinary Seaman. She had been built in Kiel, Germany in 1927, for the socially prominent, multi-millionaire publisher Colonel Ira C. Coakley, of Aurora, Illinois.

We loaded rum and cigars for the owner and his guests at Havana, Cuba, then followed a course through the Azores and arrived in Southampton, England in May 1936. We waited four-five weeks for the owner and his guests to arrive on the SS Normandie. The owner had gotten seasick crossing the Atlantic after he took delivery of the

7

Happy Days, so he always crossed on a liner. He instructed us to meet him in France. *Happy Days* made a five-month, scenic cruise to Oslo and Copenhagen. The owner and his party returned to the U.S. on the new *SS Queen Mary*, and we sailed back to Miami and Palm Beach. We later made cruises to Central America.

On reflection this job and the places I saw were the highlights of my long seagoing career. Seamanship was practiced at its finest. For example, learning to care for all the fancy work on her launches and speed boats was expected. We wore snappy uniforms because of the type of passengers aboard and were better paid than on the union ships. I learned Morse code to qualify for the additional $15.00 per month offered by the Captain, which brought my pay up to the then unheard of sum of $105.00 per month.

In a year and a half, I advanced to Senior Quartermaster and, by studying navigation, Junior Third Mate. My experiences on the *Happy Days* molded me for going to sea.

I returned home to Philadelphia for what I thought would be a brief stay before getting another ship. Instead, I got married and went into retail sales.

Before World War II, we moved to Long Beach, California because I told my wife how pretty it was there. With my background in yachts I got a job as a wire splicer in the Rigging Loft at the Terminal Island Shipyard.

When World War II broke out, my choice was to return to sea or be drafted into the Army. I entered the U.S. Maritime Service (USMS) Training School at Alameda, California and graduated in the top ten percent of my class with a Third Mate's license.

Captain George E. McCarthy, Jr.:

I was born in Monroe, New York. My father was in the Massachusetts Maritime Academy's Class of 1916 and served in the U.S. Navy in World War I. Afterward, he and my mother opened a restaurant, but had to close it when Prohibition came in. My father returned to sea, and I lived with my grandmother in Arlington, Massachusetts. He became a Master with the McCormack Steamship Company on the West Coast and then a Hull Inspector with the Bureau of Marine Inspections and Navigation. In World War II he was commissioned a Lieutenant in the U.S. Coast Guard Reserve and was a Hearing Examiner in Brisbane, Australia, New Guinea, and the Philippines. He married his Australian chauffeur, and they returned to the U.S.

My grandfather also went to sea, as a fisherman in County Cork, Ireland.

My son graduated from the Texas Maritime Academy and works ashore for a ship operator.

After I graduated from high school in June 1941, my father got me a job as an Apprentice Seaman at the USMS School at Hoffman Island, off Staten Island, New York. I learned to climb rigging and sail on the three-masted schooner *Vermer* on the East River and Long Island Sound in the cold and wet October and November of 1941.

I volunteered to go to the new, quasi-military, USMS School at St. Petersburg, Florida. We went out daily on the *Joseph Conrad*, the smallest square-rigger afloat, good training and experience. Captain Alan Villiers later sailed her around the world.

We also trained on the *SS American Seaman*, a flush decker, that is, no poop nor raised focsle. After The United States entered World War II, we painted everything gray, including the brass we had polished, and cruised in the Gulf of Mexico. Once, while docking, her forward peak tank was punctured when the ship hit the dock. We spent three days cleaning the filthy tank prior to repair. At this point I applied for admission to the U.S. Merchant Marine Academy, Kings Point, New York.

The entire crew of the *American Seaman* was transferred to New York City to go out as Ordinary

9

Seaman. Tankers were being sunk off the East Coast of the U.S., and they couldn't wait for us to get AB tickets.

While on three days' leave with my family in Massachusetts at the end of February 1942, I got my letter of appointment to Kings Point.

On March 2, 1942, I reported to the Academy, located at the Chrysler Estate at Great Neck, Long Island and lived in the greenhouse. We built barracks and did a little studying of basic courses. I got my seaman's papers and on May 6, 1942, was assigned to the *SS Mormacmoon* , a Moore-McCormack Steamship Company C-3 type cargo ship built in 1940.

We sailed in Mormac's regular liner service for the East Coast of South America. Because of the danger of German submarines we could run only during daylight - at eighteen knots to Cape Charles, Cape Henry, and Lynhaven Roads, Virginia, and Charleston and then departed for Port of Spain, Trinidad with four PT boats on deck for the British. After sighting one submarine we arrived safely.

The *Mormacmoon* called at Rio de Janeiro and Santos, Brazil; Montevideo, Uruguay; and Buenos Aires, Argentina for canned beef, hides, and bales of wool and returned to New York on July 16, 1942.

We loaded ammunition, tanks, and crated aircraft in New Jersey for the British in Suez and sailed on August 4, 1942. I'll talk later about my wartime experiences in the Middle East and Mediterranean. I got back to New York on March 6, 1943.

With a waiver, I moved up from Deck Cadet to Junior Mate, under the Second Mate, on the *SS Monterey*, a Matson Line passenger ship being operated as a troop ship for the U.S. Army Transport Service. The Matson ships were "husbanded" by Isbrandtsen Line, that is, Isbrandtsen was their agent. Hans Isbrandtsen, the line's founder and owner interviewed me for the job.

I got off in San Francisco to study for my Third Mate's license at the USMS School at San Mateo, California and obtained it in August 1943. I am in the Class of 1943 at the U.S. Merchant Marine Academy. The Academy was originally a three-year course, but I completed it in a year and a half. Many of my classmates were killed in action.

Rear Admiral Richard A. Bauman, U.S. Coast Guard (Retired):

I was born and raised in Fitchburg, Massachusetts. From my earliest memory I wanted to go to the Massachusetts Nautical School, now known as the Massachusetts Maritime Academy, at Buzzards Bay, Massachusetts and kept a scrapbook with every mention of it.

Since I was a child of the Great Depression, my parents did not have the $800.00 tuition. I graduated from high school in 1942, and worked in a machine shop to earn it.

After passing the entrance examination and interview by two instructors, I entered the Massachusetts Nautical School in November 1942. The course was sixteen months long, including six months of cruising Long Island Sound on the New York Maritime Academy's Training Ship *Empire State*. A cadet's pay was $64.00 per month. I graduated with a Third Mate's license in May 1944.

John W. Ramsey:

I went to sea with my grandfather on fishing boats and lobster boats out of Portland, Maine as a cook at age eight. He had licenses as Chief Engineer of Steam, Motor, and Sailing Vessels and had sailed around Cape Horn as a coal-passer. He told me that the money was on big ships, not fishing boats, and influenced my life a great deal. My grandfather thought that going to the Maine Maritime Academy was a good idea, but told me that, if I went into the Deck Department, not to come home. He was a product of the "wooden ships and iron men" era and lived to eighty-eight.

125 people entered Maine Maritime Academy for our indoctrination by a First Classman named Daley, an ex-Marine Corps Drill Instructor.

Every winter we took a training cruise to warmer southern waters on the Training Ship *State of Maine*.

Sixty-two or sixty-three of us graduated as Third Mates three years later, in June 1961.

Captain John W. "Jake" Schindler:

I was born and raised in Bridgeport, Connecticut. I graduated, with the author in the Class of 1962, from the State University of New York (SUNY) Maritime College, Fort Schuyler, The Bronx, New York with a Bachelor of Science (BS) degree in Marine Transportation, a Third Mate's license and $40.00 to my name.

In order to complete the 159 credits required for the bachelor's degree in four years, cadets attended classes five and a half days a week. In addition, during three, ten-week, summer cruises to Europe on the Training Ships *Empire State III and Empire State IV*, cadets attended more classes, performed ship's work, and stood watches.

Captain Douglas Glenn:

I have a seagoing heritage. My father sailed between the World Wars. My grandfather went to sea and was torpedoed off the coast of Greenland during World War II. My mother worked in the Paymaster's Office of United States Lines in New York. When family friends passed through, I heard stories from all over the world. The sea was ingrained in me, and I had the wanderlust from a young age.

I went to Admiral Farragut Academy, a Navy oriented high school in New Jersey, and then to the Maine Maritime

Academy, where I graduated with a Third Mate's license in 1964.

Captain John F. Wanner:

I was born in the Bay Ridge section of Brooklyn, New York, overlooking New York Harbor. By the time I was four years old, I could name every ship going in and out of the harbor, its owner and destination.

I graduated from the SUNY Maritime College with a B.S. degree and a Third Mate's license in April, 1967, a couple of months early because of the need for officers at the height of the Vietnam War.

Captain Gerald V. "Jerry" Smeenk:

I was born and raised in The Bronx, New York and became interested in the sea at about age thirteen through a combination of books and family friends. I read about the SUNY Maritime College, aimed for it through high school, and graduated with a B.S. degree and a Third Mate's license in 1967."

Captain Arthur H. Sulzer:

While in high school in Philadelphia, Pennsylvania I wanted to be an archeologist. My father, who graduated from the New York State Maritime Academy in 1940, was Port Engineer for the Hospital Ship *Hope*. I worked on her in the shipyard. After hearing the officers' stories, their salaries and long vacations, I decided to apply to both the U.S. Merchant Marine Academy and the SUNY Maritime College as an Engineering Cadet. I was accepted at both, but went to SUNY Maritime because my father had gone there.

The school and I parted for a semester over grades. I returned as a Deck Cadet. I have the distinction of having made two "Mug", or first, training cruises, once in the Engine Department and then in the Deck Department.

I graduated with a BS degree and a Third Mate's license in December 1974.

Teresa Olsen Preston:

The U.S. Merchant Marine Academy started accepting women in 1974. A friend at the Federal Maritime Administration asked me to apply. My intention was to minor in oceanography and go on to graduate school in marine biology, but I fell in love with sailing while a Cadet on my first ship, the SS *Export Freedom*, an American Export Lines containership running to Northern Europe. I graduated with a BS degree and a Third Mate's license in 1978.

William G. Bullock, Jr.:

I grew up in Rockville, Maryland and went to the Maine Maritime Academy, although my father, uncle and sister are graduates of the SUNY Maritime College. When I graduated in April 1986, I wanted to ship out because I like the peace and the opportunities at sea. So often maritime graduates told me that they regretted not having gone to sea.

HIRING ON

They recall their first job as an officer, a Third Mate.

Captain Carter:

Immediately after graduation from the New York Nautical School, I obtained my Third Mate's license from the Steamboat Inspection Service of the U.S. Department of Commerce. I spent Christmas at home in Milwaukee. I began looking for a job at the offices of steamship companies in New York City in January 1930, but they were scarce due to the Great Depression.

On the same day that I had been accepted as a night caretaker in a funeral parlor, I got a Third Mate's job with Isthmian Line, wholly owned by U.S. Steel, and began four years on the SS *Steel Age*. She was a "three islander," with a focsle, midship house and poop, built about 1920, 450 feet long and 10,000 deadweight tons with five cargo holds. We picked up steel in Baltimore, Philadelphia, and New York, carried it to ports on both coasts of India and returned with burlap and jute from Calcutta and a few hundred chests of tea from Colombo, Ceylon.

Commodore Alexanderson:

Jobs were hard to find because of the Depression. Through a contact of my father, in 1930, I got a three-week relief Third Mate's job sailing coastwise in the SS *Haygood*, a Cities Service tanker.

Captain Atkinson:

After graduating from the New York Nautical School in October 1933, I went to work at $30.00 a month, as a Deck

Cadet again, on the *SS Black Gull*, of Black Diamond Line. Because of their U.S. Mail contract on each ship Black Diamond had to carry two cadets who were native born U.S. citizens, so they hired many school ship graduates.

Black Diamond Line ran about ten ships from Boston, New York, Philadelphia, Baltimore, and Norfolk to Antwerp and Rotterdam. About six of them were 5029-ton Hog Islanders, built at the end of World War I at Hog Island in the Delaware River south of Philadelphia. They were perfectly flat, no camber and no sheer to the deck; ugly, but very strong ships with five hatches: two forward, one midships, and two aft, and three islands: focsle, midship house, and poop.

On the *SS Black Osprey* I progressed to Fourth Mate at $90 a month, a glorified AB, watching cargo handling, but still not standing my own sea watch.

In August 1935, I made a relief trip as Third Mate on the *SS Evelyn*, a small general cargo carrier in Bull Lines' very good U.S coastwise and Puerto Rico trade.

Captain Fowler:

After graduation from the School Ship *Annapolis* in 1931, I went directly to New York with a classmate to look for a job. We each took half of a list of steamship companies. At my first stop, Isthmian Line, I was promised an AB's job on the inbound *SS Mobile City*. I went home to wait for their call. Isthmian never called, but I had a wonderful time all summer.

Calmar Line, a subsidiary of Bethlehem Steel, offered me a job as AB on the *SS Flomar,* carrying automobiles, general cargo, and steel products in the intercoastal trade. We carried everything. I recall Number One Lower Hold full of Hershey chocolate for the West Coast.

We came back with lumber, all hand-stowed in ports from Seattle, Washington to Eureka, California. Port time was long, so a voyage took three months. I made three trips and paid off in New York thinking that I could get a berth with United States Lines. They were not hiring, so I went back home for another fine vacation.

The fall of 1933 was the lowest point in the Great Depression. I returned to New York to look for work. A new Third Mate and I stayed at the Seamen's YMCA on West 20th Street and daily walked along the Hudson and East River piers. Crowds were shaping up for jobs, but few men were ever called. After a month, with my funds very low, I moved downtown to the Seamen's Church Institute.

Calmar rehired me as an AB back on the SS Flomar, due to sail from Baltimore in two weeks.

With my limited funds I had purchased a used sextant and took sun sights on the bridge when I came off the 4 - 8 A.M. watch. At noon, I lined up with the Captain, Second and Third Mates on the wing of the bridge to take noon latitude sights. On my second trip the Captain asked me to take star sights with the Mate on the 4 - 8 A.M. watch, work out the sights and then relieve him until 8 A.M. I took evening star sights with the Mate, too. The Captain was a tough down-easter, but treated me like a son. At the end of each voyage he gave me a discharge as a higher-ranking Quartermaster. By standing watches on the SS Flomar, it wasn't long before I felt right at home. I left her to go as Third Mate on the SS Alamar. After a year, I passed the examination for Second Mate and was immediately promoted to Second Mate on the Alamar.

Captain White:

After graduating from the USMS Training School at Alameda, California at the beginning of World War II, my first Third Mate's job was on the SS Bluejacket. She was a C-2, five-hatch, ship being built for the United Fruit Company at Moore Shipbuilding and Drydock Company, Oakland, California. Her hull was very thoroughly insulated to carry "reefer," refrigerated, cargoes and had electric winches, versus the steam winches on Liberty Ships.

We carried ammunition and mustard gas to Brisbane, Australia and were all issued gas masks. I told the U.S. Army Chemical Warfare Officer aboard that chemical warfare had been banned by the Geneva Convention. He replied that the U.S. Army wanted to have chemical weapons in case the Japanese used them.

We departed Australia with "reefer" cargoes - mutton, beef and butter for England.

Captain McCarthy:

I joined Local 90 of the International Organization of Masters, Mates and Pilots (MM&P) in San Francisco after graduating from the U.S. Merchant Marine Academy in August 1943. I went on the *SS Mooremacwren*, a C-1 cargo ship, as Junior Third Mate. Unescorted and without running lights, we transported 6,000 - 8,000 U.S. Army troops from San Francisco to Espiritu Santo in the New Hebrides in twenty-two days. We carried troops to Guadalcanal after the invasion there. The stink of death was everywhere.

Merchant Mariners were not allowed ashore. Our U.S. Navy Gunnery Officer went ashore and brought back some nurses for Thanksgiving dinner. They enjoyed the showers on the ship and wanted toilet paper more than anything else. Our Captain gave them a case of it.

On arriving Fiji, we were advised by blinker light that there was a bottle of liquor for each officer at the British Forces Store. The Captain had taken my bottle because I wasn't yet 21 years old. I told him that I was old enough to have a license and was old enough to have my bottle. He gave it to me, but said that I had to drink it ashore.

British native troops embarked at Fiji. Then we loaded equipment at Espiritu Santo and arrived at Bouganville in the Solomon Islands on D-Day plus 3.

Once out of the South Pacific, we were not afraid of Japanese submarines. All the deck officers felt the strain of running without lights and no radar. I had two near collisions during my watches.

The ship got back to San Francisco on December 26, 1943. I turned 21 on December 30th and celebrated on New Year's Eve at the Palace Hotel with some Merchant Marine Academy classmates.

Admiral Bauman:

After graduating from the Massachusetts Nautical School in May, 1944, I joined Local 11 of the MM&P in Boston. The War Shipping Administration assigned me as Third Mate on the SS *Stephen C. Foster*, a Liberty Ship named after the famous composer.

My stateroom, with its settee, desk and built-in bunk, appeared palatial after the training ship.

I introduced myself to the Captain, a retired New York City ferryboat Captain. He asked me only how many trips I had made.

We loaded 8,000 tons of bombs in the holds and tanks and trucks on deck and sailed at night in a convoy bound for Halifax, Nova Scotia. During World War II ships always carried deck cargo. Prior to sailing, the Captain arrived at the ship so intoxicated that he had to be brought aboard in a litter. The Chief Mate got us underway.

At 10 P.M. on my first watch, I saw flashing red and green lights on another ship, but ignored them. When dawn broke on the Chief Mate's 4 - 8 A.M. watch, he asked where the convoy was? The flashing lights I had ignored were the Convoy Commodore's "Christmas Tree" signals to turn to a new course. We arrived Halifax alone and twenty-four hours late.

Thirty days later, a few days after the Normandy invasion, we arrived at the pilot station for Cherbourg, France. When the French Pilot learned that our cargo was bombs, he would not take us into the mined harbor. We proceeded to the area of the Normandy Beachhead. The bombs were unloaded into lighters, which took 45 days.

I got off the ship in New York and went home. For the first time in the war, I had to deal with ration cards for items such as shoes.

Mr. Ramsey:

When I graduated from the Maine Maritime Academy in June 1961, maritime strikes were going on. So I shipped out of San Francisco with the Military Sea Transportation Service (MSTS) as Junior Third Mate on an ammunition ship, the *SS Sergeant Andrew Miller*, a big Victory Ship. We loaded at Port Chicago, California and discharged at Pearl Harbor, Japan, Korea, Taiwan, Vietnam, Guam, and the Aleutian Islands. I spent a year with MSTS on two ammunition ships and the passenger ship *SS Daniel I. Sultan*. The *Sultan*, with a crew of 265, carried 2,000 troops and 500 dependents on twenty-seven-day round trips from San Francisco to Korea.

Captain Schindler:

After joining the MM&P in Providence, Rhode Island in June 1962, I lived at the YMCA. The forty dollars I had at graduation from New York Maritime ran out, and my parents wired me twenty-five more.

My first ship was the *SS Oakey L. Alexander*, a coal-burning Victory Ship built late in World War II, 450 feet long, 7750 deadweight tons, operated by the Pocohontas Fuel Company. I felt competent with all the bridge equipment. However, I had to develop confidence in my ship-handling ability as we carried coal from Norfolk to Fall River, Massachusetts. My memory is of a dingy coal boat, where my clothes were always dirty.

We then picked up a load of phosphate in Tampa, Florida for Maine. In the course of the voyage, it solidified.

After small charges of dynamite loosened it, the phosphate was bulldozed out of the holds.

Captain Glen:

Within days of graduation from the Maine Maritime Academy in 1964, I went on the *SS Remsen Heights*, an old Victory ship of American Export - Isbrandtsen Lines running to Northern Europe. After a full year as Third Mate, I got off for my Second Mate's exam, took a brief vacation, and went back on her as Second Mate. Through the end of 1965, we ran on the Bay of Biscay, English Channel, and North Sea with general cargo to ports like Santander and Bilbao, Spain; St. Nazaire and Le Havre, France; Antwerp, Rotterdam, Bremerhaven and Bremen. The fog and generally miserable weather in that part of the world, North Atlantic storms and hurricanes, with minimal navigational equipment, was my trail by fire.

Captain Smeenk:

When I graduated from the SUNY Maritime College in 1967, shipping was very good due to the Vietnam War. Every day, sixty - seventy jobs were posted in the MM&P's New York Hall.

As Third Mate on the *SS Mooremacgulf*, a C-2 cargo ship bound for the East Coast of South America with general cargo, I was alone on the bridge for the first time. On the Empire State IV, the SUNY Maritime College training ship, there were thirty - forty cadets crowded around the chronometer when shooting stars. About fifteen cadets were on the bridge at all times. On the *Mooremacgulf* I tried to apply my book knowledge under a Captain who believed that the best way to learn was to do it myself. To my discomfort, he stayed away from the bridge as much as possible.

On my next ship, an old C-2 of Central Gulf Lines, the other Third Mate, a Panama Canal tugboat Captain, transferred his great knowledge and enthusiasm for the sea to me. Outbound for thirty-four days at thirteen knots, I learned how to be a good Third Mate. It was a quiet trip, carrying ammunition from the depot at Sunny Point, South Carolina around South Africa to the Shah's army in Bandar Shahpur, Iran and foodstuffs for Bombay, India.

I took star sights on the Second Mate's watch and learned the stars' names down to the second magnitude. At the time there had been a space launch. To pass the time, I mentally calculated how many hundreds of years it would take at thirteen knots to reach the moon. I don't remember the result and no longer have the time on watch to do the calculation.

Captain Wanner:

I graduated from the SUNY Maritime College in April 1967, at the height of the Vietnam War, and joined the MM&P in New York a few days later.

My first ship was the *SS Pioneer Mist*, an old Mariner class ship of United States Lines, in liner service to the Far East. We sailed in the evening while I was on the 8 - 12 watch. At Ambrose Light the Pilot got off. The Captain pointed her south and said, "You got it." Over twenty years and 2,000,000 miles later, I'm still alive, so I must have done something right.

The container era was beginning, but the high-value televisions, tape recorders, and sewing machines we loaded in Japan were hand-stowed one box at a time.

Shipping was so busy that you couldn't sign off a ship.

Captain Sulzer:

After graduating from the SUNY Maritime College with a Third Mate's license in December 1974, my first job was Staff Duty Officer there. I was a Watch Officer on SUNY Maritime's Training Ship *Empire State V* for the 1975 summer cruise to Scotland and Barcelona, Spain.

I then became Third Mate on the *SS Exxon Houston*, a 795-foot, 65,000-ton tanker, built in the late-1960s, carrying refined petroleum products, like gasoline, from Houston to Philadelphia. I worked two months on and then had two months off. She went aground off Hawaii in 1989, and was scrapped.

Ms. Preston:

When I graduated from the U.S. Merchant Marine Academy in 1978, seagoing jobs were easy to get, particularly for women. I applied only to tanker firms, got three offers, and went with Exxon as Third Mate on the *SS Exxon Boston*. She was built in 1960, 743 feet long, 40,000 tons, and carried 300,000 - 350,000 barrels of up to six grades of products. With a beam of 105 feet, she had been built to barely squeeze through the Panama Canal.

Exxon used its U.S. flag tankers in the U.S. coastwise trade and its foreign-flag ships in the overseas trade because it was cheaper. I made a seventy-day trip tramping from Texas and Baton Rouge, Louisiana via the Panama Canal to San Francisco, Washington, Long Beach, California and back to Philadelphia.

I decided that tankers were more exciting than general cargo ships because of having control in pumping their cargoes, rather than just counting boxes in or out of the ship.

Mr. Bullock:

When I graduated from the Maine Maritime Academy in April 1986, I wanted to ship out because I like the peace and opportunities to learn at sea. So often maritime graduates had told me that they regretted not having gone to sea.

I tried to join the Marine Engineers Beneficial Association District II (MEBA II) in Brooklyn, New York. They were not accepting new members, unless you would first work on a fleet of survey ships under contract to the U.S. Navy. With this vague promise of union membership, I went as Third Mate on the U.S. Naval Ship (USNS) *Vindicator*, built in 1985, 224 feet and 1492 tons, with a crew of 22.

For 120 days, with a one-day mid-mission refueling stop in Scotland, *Vindicator* did survey work in the North Atlantic. I stood the 8 - 12 watch twice a day at a salary of $72.00 per day. There was no mail or contact with family.

When I didn't get my union book at the end of the trip, I obtained a Certificate in Crude Oil Washing and Inert Gas systems at MEBA II's School in Dania, Florida and looked for work on non-union tankers.

LINER SERVICE

Steamship companies maintaining regularly scheduled freight services to or from one or more ports are called liners or liner services, as opposed to tramp operators, or tramps, who do not maintain regular schedules and pursue cargo contracts anywhere.

Captain Carter:

In 1934, I became Second Mate on Isthmian Lines' *SS Steel Trader*. We loaded steel in U.S East Coast ports for Los Angeles, San Francisco, Portland, and Seattle and returned two months later with timber, prefabricated doors, and canned fruit. It was cheaper to ship Midwest steel by rail to the East Coast and then by ship to the West Coast than directly by rail to the West Coast. This trade ended for Isthmian when Kaiser built steel mills on the West Coast.

The *Steel Trader* also carried steel from New York to Hawaii for cans and returned with sugar and pineapple. In this trade the perfect outbound freight combination was found - sheet steel and automobiles, using all the weight and cubic capacity of the ship.

In Isthmian's India service the trip up the Hugeley River to Calcutta was a day's run in daylight. The Indian Pilot, wearing whites, came aboard with a servant boy carrying his trunk and of suitcases. While we waited for the right stage of the tide, the boy provided whatever items the pilot needed. He even lit the pilot's cigarette before transferring it to the pilot's cigarette holder.

On return trips from India we sometimes carried elephants, pythons, and monkeys for Frank "Bring 'Em Back Alive" Buck's circus. When asked what I knew about carrying elephants, I replied, "A lot more than when I started."

Each python was fed a goat before loading and digested it during the voyage. Because they were shipped "In Care of Chief Mate" I had to regularly sprinkle water on them.

Cages holding twenty-five monkeys each were stowed on deck. I fed them every day. Once, in Port Said, Egypt, they escaped. Some jumped overboard, and others climbed the masts and rigging or swung on pipes in the engine room. We put on our own circus.

A load of mongoose we carried to Hawaii was not permitted to land and was shipped back to India.

In the British Royal Mail tradition ships flying the mail flag got preference as far as pilots and docking. We had about a hundred bags of low priority U.S. mail aboard approaching Port Said. I ran up our U.S. mail flag, and the ship was able to dock immediately.

In my time at sea we had no electronic navigation equipment, like radar and radio direction finder. We did have gyrocompasses on the Isthmian ships from their beginning because cargoes of steel caused great inaccuracies in magnetic compasses. With no fathometer, we dropped a deep sea lead with a glass tube to determine the depth of the water by changes in pressure.

Commodore Alexanderson:

Through my father's contacts, Captain Donnelly, the Marine Superintendent of Isthmian Lines, hired me as a Third Mate *in* the *SS Knoxville City* on August 1, 1930. I say *in* the *SS Knoxville City*. People say *on* ships, but that's wrong.

She was a one of a type of good ships built about 1922 by U.S. Steel, owners of Isthmian Lines, at their yards in Anniston and Mobile, Alabama and in liner service from New York to India. They were over 400 feet long, about 8,000 tons, and made twelve knots. Hatch number five was in an uncovered well deck. Two large doors at the after end of hatch number four could be removed, which reduced the cubic capacity of the ship and the tolls paid in the Panama and Suez Canals.

These ships were the first to have gyro compasses because of the effects of the steel cargoes on magnetic compasses. In some there was a separate room for the gyro. In others it was at the after end of the saloon, or officers' dining room.

We were in liner service to India. I transferred to the *SS Fairfield City* as Third Mate, then to the *SS Steel Engineer* as Second Mate. Promotions were slow. Even after getting Chief Mate's and Master's licenses, I was still sailing as Second Mate in 1936.

During my seven-year, World War II Navy service, I had commands. My first United States Lines command was the *SS American Forwarder*, a C-2 on the "Whiskey Run," picking up cargoes of whisky in Liverpool, Glasgow, Dublin, and Belfast for Boston and New York.

After the passenger liner *SS United States* was laid-up in 1969, I went as Master of United States Lines' *SS American Legion*, making one-month round-trips from New York to the United Kingdom, Amsterdam, and Germany. She was a Mariner of the Lancer Class, extended to about 600 feet while still under construction in 1969, with a capacity of 1250 twenty-foot containers including reefers.

Although I had last been in a cargo ship over fifteen years earlier, when they were break-bulk, I had no trouble adjusting to containerization. Pilferage was greatly reduced on container ships. However, in some instances entire containers were stolen.

U.S. Lines' northern European trade was extended, first by a two-month trip from New York to San Pedro and Oakland, California, Honolulu, Hong Kong, Kobe and Yokohama, Japan, and then to Honolulu, Guam and Hong Kong. We would arrive back in New York in the morning, load, and sail the next morning. After two trips, I got a trip off. As shipping slowed down, it became one trip on and one trip off.

Captain Atkinson:

I wasn't interested in a steady job, but in enjoying myself and seeing the world. When I was down to my last $10, I'd ship out as AB.

In 1936, I was AB on the 7917-ton *SS Edward Luckenbach*. Luckenbach was a big operator, with about twenty-seven ships in intercoastal service.

To get back to the East Coast after the long 1936 maritime strike, I shipped as AB on Calmar Line's *SS Portmar*, bound for Boston with a cargo of lumber. She was a slow and unwieldy ship and a bad feeder. Her Master, Captain Buchanan, offered me a Third Mate's job. I turned it down and continued to Baltimore on Calmar's *SS Pennmar*.

I got my Second Mate's license in 1937, but couldn't find a berth. Bull Line hired seamen to work on their ships in port at $3.00 per day, so I did that for a while.

On May 6, 1937, I went as Quartermaster on the *SS F.J. Luckenbach*, about 14,000 tons, eight hatches with thirty-two booms.

The following September, the company sent me to the *SS Florence Luckenbach* as Third Mate. She was built in 1919, sunk, was salvaged, and was the slowest ship in Luckenbach's fleet. On a run from Gulf of Mexico to the West Coast she had lots of port time, which I liked. After only two trips off, I moved up to Second Mate in July 1939. She was my home until 1941.

In August 1940, we were taken off the intercoastal run to load a full cargo of steel and gasoline in drums for Yokohama, Japan. The crew staged a job action in San Pedro, California to protest taking war materials to Japan. The company salved its conscience by giving us extra pay for the voyage.

After discharging in Yokohama, we took a full cargo of rubber from Saigon to New York. There, under charter to Isthmian Lines, we loaded general cargo for the Persian

Gulf - Bahrain; Khorramshahr, Bandar e-Shahpur and Abadan, Iran and Basra, Iraq.

After carrying a full cargo of cement from Karachi to Bandar e-Shahpur, several of us were hospitalized in Abadan for treatment of malaria.

We loaded at Calcutta and Colombo, Ceylon for New York, where I got off in November 1941, fifteen months after the voyage began. On her next voyage, the *Florence Luckenbach* was torpedoed in the Indian Ocean, but there were no casualties.

Captain Fowler:

In 1955, I decided to return to sea. The Personnel Officer of the Calmar Line in New York had graduated from the Pennsylvania School Ship *Annapolis* some years after me and offered me a Chief Mate's job. Because my navigation was rusty after three years ashore, I told him that I wanted to sail as Third Mate.

After several intercoastal trips as Third Mate and Second Mate, I became Chief Mate. To me the Chief Mate's job was more important than the Master's on those ships. When I had been Master, I always spent a lot of time taking navigational sights and doing paper work. On the Calmar vessels I never saw a Master with a sextant in his hand nor making up payrolls.

My wife and I always rented a summer cottage on Kent Island, Maryland. I was Chief Mate discharging lumber in Providence, Rhode Island. The Personnel Officer asked me to relieve the Master, so that he could go on vacation. I told him that my vacation had been approved, I had a deposit on a cottage, my wife's health was not good, and I really wanted to be relieved. I got my vacation, but Calmar never again offered me a Master's job.

When I was Chief Mate on the *SS Marymar*, a large rebuilt C-4 vessel, the Master became ill after leaving Panama. I arranged with the company to anchor in Acapulco, Mexico. About ten officials, one of them a doctor, boarded the ship. They took the Master, and many cartons of our cigarettes, ashore. I proceeded to Long Beach with all my papers ready for arrival from a foreign port. Calmar's shore staff at Long Beach thought that I would certainly continue as Master. A day later, a Master I had never heard of arrived from the East Coast. When the voyage ended back in Baltimore, I paid off.

After several weeks at home, the Personnel Officer begged me to take one of two vacant Third Mate's job on a ship ready to sail. He promised to pay me off in Long Beach and fly me home to Baltimore for a Chief Mate's job on another ship. No relief appeared in Long Beach. We continued up the coast. The other Third Mate showed up in Seattle, but Calmar did not fly me home as promised. I paid off in Baltimore.

Captain White:

After World War II, I knew that I wanted to stay in big ships. I sailed out of San Francisco with American South African Line, later known as Farrell Lines. There I met up again with the *SS Frank Adair Monroe*, a Liberty Ship I had commanded in the South Pacific.

In the early 1950s, I worked for American President Lines making four-month, around-the-world trips westbound from San Francisco. This was difficult when raising two children, so I began to take various shorter jobs out of the MM&P Halls.

In the mid-1950s, I went with Isthmian Line, a fleet of twenty-four, nice C-3s, boom ships, in four months' around-the-world service.

Loading steel in Baltimore one day, I saw the *SS Christos M*, my old *SS Frank Adair Monroe*, laid up in a nest of Liberty Ships.

On these trips I got one day in my homeport of Long Beach and sailed again. After a year with Isthmian, I got a month's vacation.

Then I went with Calmar Line, a subsidiary of U.S. Steel, out of New York. I was Chief Mate on an intercoastal run, with steel outbound and lumber back. It was like the old Shepherd Line for me. I found the job very enjoyable, but, for seniority reasons, never sailed as Master.

Captain McCarthy:

In December 1945, the Port Captain of Moore McCormack Steamship Company in New York ordered me to the *SS Clearwater Victory* as Chief Mate. She was about 500 feet long and fast, eighteen and a half knots from 8,500 horsepower steam turbines. The Master was C.W. Spear, from Maine, one of the finest Masters, navigators, and ship handlers I ever met. I was Chief Mate with him on about six ships, and we're still friends. His only vice was his love of ice cream.

We arrived in Philadelphia on December 13, 1945, to load for Mooremac's liner service to South America. My wife joined me.

Under Captain Olie Johnson, on January 5, 1946 we sailed for Buenos Aires, Argentina; Rio de Janiero and Santos, Brazil, and Montevideo, Uruguay. After discharging, we loaded for the West Coast.

In Buenos Aires about forty Japanese civilians interned during World War II, embarked for return to Japan via California. I put the men in the Gun Crew's Quarters aft and the women and children in the midship house. Language was a problem, but one of the men spoke English.

Six Japanese flags were painted on the *Clearwater Victory* for the six Japanese planes her crew shot down during the war. Mooremac instructed that the flags be painted over, which bothered the ship's crew.

There were no problems at sea, but the Japanese could not go ashore due to customs and immigration regulations in each port. Entering the Panama Canal we were met by U.S. aircraft, patrol boats, and a destroyer. U.S. Army and Navy intelligence officers boarded the ship and interviewed them. Guards kept the Japanese in their quarters, so that they couldn't see the canal. On April 11, 1946, they disembarked at Long Beach, California.

I met my father, whom I had last seen in 1942, and his Australian bride. He was assigned as a Commander at the U.S. Coast Guard Base in Long Beach.

I left the ship because it was staying on the West Coast and chartered a DC-3 from Flying Tiger Airline for the crew to fly from Oakland to New York. It was a military aircraft with seats along the sides and no heat. At 3 A.M. in Albuquerque I tried to buy flight insurance, but couldn't because the airline was unscheduled. We were dropped in Newark, New Jersey, and I flew to Boston on a regularly scheduled flight. A high school classmate of mine was the stewardess.

On June 3, 1946, I reported to the Mooremac's SS *Beatrice Victory* as Chief Mate. The Master was my friend Captain Spear. The Junior Third Mate was Jim Crowley, who later became Executive Vice President of Mooremac. Jim and I are still friends.

At this time, a week to ten days in each South American port was not unusual. My wife made her first airplane flight to join me in Jacksonville, Florida. Life was good!

After a maritime strike in the U.S., we began loading for South America at Chester and Philadelphia, Pennsylvania on September 23, 1946.

From October 11 until November 4, 1946, we were anchored in Santos, Brazil waiting for a dock. Such delays were common due to congestion in the port.

On this voyage we entered the port of Rio Grande del Sol at the mouth of Lago dos Patros, Lake of Ducks, a large, shallow lake leading to Porto Alegre, Brazil. Porto Alegre was a well-run port with a large German population. It wasn't part of the regular run, but we sometimes loaded wheat and grain in Rio Grande del Sol and canned meats from the Armor and Swift packing houses in Porto Alegre. The shallow lake restricted the ship's draft.

Barges were used for loading, discharging, or storage in many South American ports. Mooremac had their own steel barges, with rolling hatches, built in the U.S. We carried them down as deck cargo, one forward and one aft, about 1946. Mooremac tugs moved the barges from the ports to their shallow water destinations. Each barge was home to a Barge Captain and his family.

I've made every port in Brazil, including little ports like Angra dos Reis, and went up the Amazon River countless times in the two years that I was in the Northern Brazil trade for Mooremac.

I completed my Master's license in Boston on March 16, 1947. The U.S. Coast Guard Officer in Charge signed it on March 17th, St. Patrick's Day, because of my Irish name. Mooremac insisted that we get as much schooling as possible, so I went to schools for Loran, gyrocompass and radar.

On March 29, 1947, I received a plum assignment, Chief Officer on the brand-new *SS Mooremacisle*, a C-3 built at Pascagoula, Mississippi, 8500 horsepower, with 90,000 cubic feet of reefer space. I was young to be the Mate on such a ship. The Master, Harry Sadler, had been Master of Mooremac's flagship, the *SS Brazil*. The *Brazil* was then in the shipyard, so the *Mooremacisle* was considered Mooremac's flagship.

We carried expensive edible oils in the deep tanks and general cargo to and from Trinidad, Bahia, Rio de Janiero, Santos, Montevideo, and Buenos Aires. The twelve passenger berths were always full both ways because no passenger ships were running.

I was still on the *Mooremacisle* in December 1947, when my daughter was born. Mooremac was like a family. My wife would meet me for dinner in a U.S. port and leave our daughter asleep in my room. The Night Mate would check on her. On another ship in another U.S. port someone would do the same for his children. My daughter took her first steps on a Mooremac ship.

By April 1948, jobs were scarce. I went on the *SS Mooremacray* as Second Mate. From the shipyard we went south in Mooremac's Mainline Service to Brazil, Uruguay, and Argentina. We continued on to the west coast of the U.S., where the *Mooremacray* temporarily joined the six Mooremac ships in service from the west coast of the U.S. to the east coast of South America. I left the ship at San Francisco on August 1, 1948.

During the Peron regime, on the *SS Mooremacray* and *SS Mooremacdale* we had to wait for sixty - ninety days for a berth in Rio de Janiero.

In the Northern Brazil trade the first port southbound was Belem. We continued south, loading and discharging in sixteen ports as far south as Recife. Northbound, we loaded and discharged in the same ports as far as Belem. The ship arrived in each port at or before dawn and sailed by nightfall. On this run we didn't get as far south as the fun ports. All cargo stowage was "optional," meaning it could be changed because our U.S. destinations were not yet determined.

The Amazon Bar at the Intercontinental Hotel in Belem was a bit of heaven because it had air conditioning and cold Brazilian beer.

At Belem we picked up Mooremac's Amazon River pilots, Claudio Lima and his two brothers. They were well paid by Brazilian standards and also got liquor, cigarettes and clothes. There were no charts, no aids to navigation, and the Amazon's channels changed all the time. The ships in this trade were were highly-maneuverable, twin diesel-powered C1-Bs running at full ahead. We ran day and night for five days going up the river and three days going down. The officers had no clue where we were, yet, to my knowledge, there was never a grounding.

During the spring flood only the pilot could tell which was the main river and which was a dead-end offshoot. His orders for course changes sometimes seemed to be away from the main channel. We frequently collided with huge tree trunks floating downriver, and the ship shuddered all over. Once one of the brothers was ill. His replacement pilot had a seizure on the bridge. The Third Mate almost had one, too.

In one port, going down river from Manaus we would point the ship's bow to the bank, drop both anchors, go aground and make bow lines fast on the bank. The stern remained in deep water with the propeller slowly turning. After loading cargo from barges, we went "Full Astern" on the engines to haul the ship back to the anchors, raised them, and turned the ship down river.

Manaus is on the Rio Negro, so called because the water is black, where it meets the Amazon River. The water is so deep that the anchor cannot be dropped. The ship tied up to a mooring buoy. A Peruvian Navy barge brought raw materials over from Iquitos, Peru for loading. Smaller ships used the dock, which had a hinge so that it could rise and fall with the spring floods.

The Manaus opera house featured big stars during the rubber boom, when Europeans, Ford, and Firestone had plantations there. It's a very old city and not particularly interesting, but, for some reason, it became a major tourist attraction.

We loaded crude rubber in balls, five-gallon cans of shelled cashews, mahogany, each piece lettered and numbered, and rosewood. Our most important cargo was 1,000 - 1,500 tons of Brazil nuts. They were stowed in paper-lined bins in the upper tween decks of the ship's three forward hatches, which were cracked for ventilation. The freight for these nuts was $125 per ton, a tremendous rate in the late-1940s.

Ten to twelve Brazilian nut trimmers, under Foreman Clavo Nasciemento, turned the nuts continually during the voyage to prevent the shells from turning white. I called them Clavo Nasciemento and his Nut Trimmer Band. They weren't paid much, but enjoyed the ship's food.

We always entered San Luis de Maranao on the flood tide and dropped both anchors. A tug dropped an anchor with manila lines attached to our ship's stern. When the tide went out, we were sitting in a little puddle surrounded by land. We quickly loaded and discharged with barges to depart by the next high tide. The climate there was too hot for beds, so the local people slept in hammocks.

I did not stand a watch on this ship because there was no time. Every day I was up before dawn for arrival, worked cargo all day, secured the ship for sailing, slept at night while underway, and started again the next day. The Captain stayed up all night and slept during the day.

In the Northern Brazil trade we occasionally made Bahia, the former capitol of Brazil. Bahia has 365 churches, one for each day of the year.

Four Mooremac C-1 vessels made round trips from New York every month to northern Brazil. Roads were almost non-existent, and railroads were poor, so ships were the major means of transport. After two years, I had enough of the tropics. I went in Mooremac's Scandinavian service on the SS *Mooremacpine*, an 8,500 horsepower Victory Ship, on November 1, 1949.

I was later Navigator on Mooremac's passenger liner SS *Brazil.*

Captain McCarthy advanced to Staff Captain on the Brazil and left the sea in 1956. From 1957 to 1987, he worked for the Federal Maritime Administration, including service as Maritime Attaché at U.S. Embassies in Paris and Buenos Aires. He received the U.S. Coast Guard's Distinguished Public Service Award for his volunteer work in getting veterans' status for U.S. Merchant Mariners' wartime service. Captain George E. McCarthy, Jr. died in March 1992, at age 70.

Admiral Bauman:

After World War II, I got my Chief Mate's license and continued sailing for Agwi Lines. Agwi stood for Atlantic, Gulf and West Indies and was a combination of older U.S. steamship companies. My first Chief Mate's job we loaded phosphate at Boca Raton, Florida right into the former troop quarters of the Liberty Ship *SS Luther Martin* and took it to Japan.

Agwi's fleet peaked at 99 ships during the war, but was declining as ships were laid up. Wartime Chief Mates were sailing as Third Mates, and Masters were Second Mates. I had no seniority with Agwi, so went looking for a job elsewhere. I lived at the Seamen's Church Institute in New York City, but carried my sextant with me for fear of theft. At every steamship company I met men carrying sextants.

I tried the U.S. Army's Military Sea Transportation Service (MSTS) in Brooklyn, New York in 1947, but no jobs were open.

I got a Junior Third Mate's job on a U.S. Lines C-2 from the east coast to the United Kingdom and Germany. The cargoes were beer and radios for the recreation of U.S. troops. On the return trip the upper tween deck was filled with cases of Scotch whiskey, so we had highly pilferable cargoes both ways.

Dotty and I married in June 1948. Since I got only two weeks' vacation, I had to quit U.S. Lines for our honeymoon.

Mr. Ramsey:

In May 1962, I joined American Export Lines (AEL) as Third Mate on the *SS Express*, a seven-hatch C-3, sailing from their Hoboken, New Jersey headquarters to India. To fill jobs engineers had been Shanghai'd from AEL's passenger ships, the *Independence* and *Constitution*.

Because the ship hadn't been stored properly, we ran out of meat almost immediately. I remember lots of sandwiches of either catsup or peanut butter.

The trip went as far as Chittagong, in Bangladesh. Under a new contract we loaded jute for carpet backing. In Madras, India the jute caught fire. We fought the fire by pouring water into the *Express'* forward cargo holds. On the second day the weight of water in the ship caused her to roll fourteen degrees toward the dock. Our National Maritime Union crew reacted to this emergency by jumping ashore or overboard. The Purser and the Chief Steward tried to launch the offshore lifeboat. We officers continued to fight the fire in six-hour shifts for ten days. All but three crewmembers left for a hotel uptown.

The fire knocked out electrical power to the forward cargo booms. On arrival back in Hoboken the water-damaged cargo was discharged using shore cranes. The *Express* went into a Wehauken, New Jersey shipyard for repairs.

I had the option of staying on the *Express* or going around the world on one of the fourteen ships of Isbrandtsen Line, which had just merged with AEL. I jumped at the chance and have made twenty-three voyages around the world. Loading and unloading a ship three times in four months at sea is "steamboatin' " at its best.

My first Isbrandtsen ship was a C-2, the *SS Flying Gull*. The author was the other Third Mate. The Skipper was Captain John McLean, nicknamed "Iron John" because in North Atlantic storms he stood on the bridge for days at a time. At age fourteen he was a sandhog working with his father on New York's Holland Tunnel. As a Navy officer in World War II McLean had a couple of mine sweepers blown out from under him. The Chief Mate was Henry Lexius, like a character from a slapstick movie. The twelve passengers were a varied lot - quiet to boisterous, pleasant to whiny, and inquisitive to bored. They saw about fifteen ports in four months for $1,600.

The most eventful part of the voyage was our collision with a Greek ore carrier, the *SS Batus*, leaving Kobe, Japan. I was on watch, relieving Second Mate Leo Valentius for supper. The *Gull* had the right of way. Instead of a Half Astern bell, the *Batus* got a Half Ahead bell on her turbo electric engine and headed for us. Captain McLean took the conn from the pilot and almost succeeded in turning the *Gull* away. *Batus* hit us on the port side of Number One hatch above the water line at the upper tween deck, pushing us over about fifteen degrees. As collision became imminent the Chief Mate and the Bosun ran back from the bow. A Mercedes stowed in the upper tween deck escaped damage by inches. After a week of repairs in a Kobe shipyard, the voyage continued eastward.

At the time my brother was a midshipman on Maine Maritime Academy's training ship cruising on the West Coast of the U.S. I hoped to rendezvous him, but the closest I came was sighting the *TS State of Maine* along the Mexican coast.

My next ship was the *SS Flying Hawk*, a sister to the *Flying Gull*. I was again shipmates with John McLean, demoted to Chief Mate. We carried cargoes ranging from circuses to locomotives around the world.

I went on another C-2, the *SS Flying Enterprise II*, named after Isbrandtsen's storied *SS Flying Enterprise*. *Flying Enterprise II* was commanded by Captain Heinrich Kurt Carlsen, famous for remaining alone aboard his *Flying Enterprise* for a week before she sank in the North Atlantic in the 1950s.

My work with Chief Mates on cargo plans was noticed by AEL's Port Captain and helped get me a Second Mate's job on the Isbrandtsen ships.

Later, I became Chief Mate on an old AEL ship, the six-hatch *SS Extavia*, in Great Lakes to the Mediterranean service. Her Captain Lore was nicknamed "Lucky" because he was so unlucky with weather. One crossing, from Lisbon to New York, took nineteen days and resulted in extensive cargo and structural damage.

I asked AEL's Personnel Manager, Tom Collins, for experience on the newer, automated ships. To get it I had to drop back to Second and Third Mate on two "A" ships, *Export Ambassador* and *Export Adventurer*, going to the Far East.

Collins promoted me to Relieving Chief Mate on one of AEL's newest ships, the *SS Export Champion*, running from the East Coast of the U.S. to the Far East. The run was called "a Japanese Coastwise," because of the number of loading and discharge ports in Japan made in ten - fifteen days. The *Champion* was a C-4, had improved Ebel cargo gear and was a real working ship. As Chief Mate I continually dealt with the problems of cargo stowage and ship's stability and trim.

I stayed on the *Export Champion* for over ten years and got along well with all of her skippers. One of the best came off AEL's passenger liners, Captain John Pershing McKenna, a gentlemen from Boston.

When Farrell Lines took over AEL in the 1970s, the ship that most impressed them was the *Export Champion*.

Captain Glen:

During 1972, I was Second Mate on American Export Lines' *SS Export Ambassador, Export Bay* and *Export Challenger,* known within the company as the "A, B, and C" ships.

Then I began eight years as Second Mate and Chief Mate in AEL's India Service on the seven-hatch *SS Exbrook*. Without air conditioning, that first trip was not pleasant.

While the Suez Canal was closed, we went around the Cape of Good Hope. After taking on bunkers at Durban, South Africa, we discharged military cargo at Diego Garcia in the Indian Ocean, where 600 U.S. Navy Seabees were building a base.

For the India run we loaded extensively on the east coast and the Gulf - Mobile, Tampa, Galveston, Houston, and New Orleans, before going foreign from New York. Outports included Karachi, Bombay, the Malabar Coast - Mangalore, Cochin, Colombo in Sri Lanka; the East Coast of India - Madras, Masulipatnam, Calcutta, and Chittagong, and Chalna in Bangladesh.

On the first few trips I mentally anguished over the horrors of life in India and wondered how people could live in such abject misery and still find contentment with their lives. Over time my eyes were opened, and I came to appreciate India's unique culture.

Voyages to India meant operational problems and weeks of delays. For instance, it was necessary to discharge cargoes into lighters to lighten the ship enough to get up the Hugeley River to Calcutta.

AEL also had trade routes to Northern Europe, the Mediterranean, the Far East, and around the world. The Mediterranean was sub-divided into Spain - Alicante, Cartagena and Malaga; Italy - Genoa, Livorno, Naples; and Marseilles, France. The Mediterranean was a "Romance Run" and much sought after by the crews.

AEL's eastern Mediterranean run made ports in the Adriatic Sea - Trieste and Brindisi, Italy; Rijeka and Split, Yugoslavia; Piraeus, Greece; Istanbul, Turkey; Burgas, Bulgaria; and Constanta, Romania.

Least desirable was the North African run - Casablanca, Algiers, Tunisia, Libya, and Alexandria and Port Said, Egypt. Traveling like a tourist from Casablanca to see Rabat and Marrakech in Morocco was fun. Conditions in the ports got worse as we went east, but I always enjoyed Beirut's fabulous Casino Libon .

As the number of ships decreased, jobs became scarce. I sailed Second Mate for a few years. In 1975, I went as Chief Mate on AEL's "B" ships, *Export Buyer* and *Export Builder*,and on a container ship, the *SS Stag Hound*, to Northern Europe.

I resumed going to India as Chief Mate on the *SS Export Adventurer.* The "A" ships, *Export Adventurer, Export Aide, Export Agent, and Export Ambassador* carried twelve passengers. They were usually retirees with the money and time to go to offbeat places, for cargo by inducement only, and who didn't care about schedule changes. Many of them were world travelers with more sea time that I. They were self-sufficient, readers and hobbyists, and didn't expect me to be their Social Director. They added civility to the trips, and I'm still friends with some.

Captain Smeenk:

After obtaining my Second Mate's license, I began sailing for Isthmian Lines, a wholly owned subsidiary of States Marine Lines, in 1969. During four years of massive U.S. Agency for International Development (USAID) shipments, we carried food supplies, like wheat, to India. Return cargoes from Chittagong and Chalna were Hessian cloth for carpet backing, in three-foot wide rolls twelve - fourteen feet long, tea, cashews, and Indian-manufactured clothes.

In the mid-1970s, I got experience with refrigerated fruits and vegetables in Prudential Lines', formerly Grace Line, regular service from the West Coast of South America to the East Coast of the U.S. Very high value cargo, like shrimp and prawns, was carried from large farms in Ecuador in freezer containers stowed on deck at a freight rate of $6,000 per forty-foot container.

In April 1979, I got a Chief Mate's job with Lykes Brothers Steamship Company, Incorporated, of New Orleans. About eighteen of Lykes twenty-nine ships had traditional booms for handling cargo. The owners called them Pacers. I spent the bulk of my career on them - the last of the boom ships in the U.S. merchant fleet. Each ship was 22,000 tons, 592 feet long and sixty-nine feet wide. All were built in the periods 1960 to 1963 and 1964 to 1966.

Four hatches were forward of the two midship houses. Number Four held forty-foot containers. Number Five was between the houses, and Number Six was aft of them. The hatches were covered by steel, hydraulic hatch covers, except the container hatch, which was covered by three twelve-ton pontoons. The booms, topping lift wires and schooner and vang guy wires were all rigged to electric winches. Three crew members could secure the ship for sea in an hour compared to fifteen crew members in eight hours for booms rigged with rope and hatches covered with boards and tarpaulins. Thefts of rope by poor stevedores were eliminated.

Lykes operated from the U.S. Gulf and East Coast to Northern Europe, the Mediterranean, Africa, and the West Coast of South America. I ran mostly to the Mediterranean, but also to the West Coast of South America, and to South, East, and Equatorial Africa on the *SS Shirley Lykes, Zoella Lykes, Letitia Lykes, Jean Lykes and Marjorie Lykes.*

We carried USAID cargoes outbound and returned empty due to the discrimination against old ships. An occasional return cargo was pallets of dowels from Tanjongmani, Brunei for use as broomsticks.

Captain Sulzer:

I wanted to see the world and try different ships, so I went with American Export Lines as Third Mate in 1977. My first ship was the *SS Export Adventurer* followed by the *Export Aide.* Both were built about 1960, 17,000 - 18,000 tons, 565 feet long, with five hatches.

In liner service, we spent three - four weeks loading on the U.S. East Coast. Occasionally we loaded partial grain cargoes at U.S. Gulf ports. With worldwide economic development, AEL carried industrial tanks, machinery, and locomotives. Much of this cargo was oversized, stowed on

43

deck, and discharged with our fifty-ton heavy lift boom. USAID cargoes included birth control devices. After loading coastwise, we returned to New York, signed foreign articles, embarked our twelve passengers, and sailed for India.

I was on the first American ship to transit the Suez Canal when it was reopened. Authorities in Alexandria, Egypt checked the ship's logbook to see that we had not called at an Israeli port on the voyage. Any ship calling in Israel could not use the canal. Ships sunk during the Arab Israeli War were still in the canal. Only the stack of a Farrell Lines ship, the *African Dawn*, I think, was visible above the water. Both banks of the canal were littered with wreckage.

We discharged at Karachi and ports on both coasts of India, like Cochin, Allepey and Quilon, and ended the outbound voyage in Calcutta.

At this point AEL made the decision whether to load a ship for an inbound voyage or continue to the Far East. I never made a trip onward and would still like to sail around the world.

Stopping at Colombo, Ceylon, now Sri Lanka, both outbound and inbound was like making a recreational port. We could drink in Colombo, unlike the Indian prohibition on alcohol except in seamen's clubs.

A couple of times we went upriver to Mumgla, Bangladesh, an anchorage in the jungle, to load jute for carpet backing. The natives lived in grass huts, used dugout canoes, and fascinated the archeologist in me. I traded them bars of soap for clay pots. Later, they offered me boatloads of clay pots. Maybe I started a cottage industry for them.

On the Indian rivers pirates came aboard using grappling hooks, stole anything they could, and got away in motor boats. Patrols on deck deterred them with fire hoses and baseball bats.

44

Since construction of a new port in Calcutta, ships no longer have to contend with sand bars and waiting for the next tidal bore to get up the Hugeley River.

Crowding in Bombay sometimes meant a boring one - two week wait at anchor to enter the locks of the port.

AEL's India trips were scheduled for ninety days, but took a minimum of one hundred days. One took 180 days and required re-provisioning. That was a real bargain for passengers.

The Second Cook being diagnosed with syphilis en route home caused one voyage delay. We anchored at Madras, India, and Health Service officials boarded. Since he was a cook, they gave everyone a blood test. All tests were negative, but upset the passengers.

The "A" ships were modified to handle up to 300 containers in two holds and on deck, for Karachi, Bombay and Calcutta. Containers were not common in this part of the world, and the ports did not have cranes. Our ten-ton booms and a couple of twenty-ton booms took the twenty-foot containers. The forty-foot containers were loaded in the vicinity of the forward and aft jumbo booms, or two twenty-ton booms were "married" to handle them. I am fortunate to have had this experience with "stick," or boom, ships.

I saw my first Russian ship in Bombay in 1977. By 1979, I saw more than a dozen. Because they did not participate in any steamship conferences, the Russians took over this trade with lower freight rates.

AEL carried progressively lower value cargoes as containerization took over. The ships were filled with USAID give-away cargoes. High value cargoes, like Ceylonese tea, went to foreign-flag ships, while we carried jute and manhole covers. U.S. ship owners wanted to continue carrying tea in chests subject to breakage. At fifteen knots they were only a few knots faster than the ships carrying tea to the Boston Tea Party.

Tea is now shipped in containers, as are all breakable, pilferable cargoes. Before containerization, we carried sneakers in boxes to New York. At the end of their shift the stevedores walked down the gangway in new white sneakers. We found their old sneakers on the beams in the hold.   Philadelphia stevedores went through the sneakers discarded by the stevedores in New York.

I made two trips on AEL's *SS Export Freedom*, 700 feet long and built as a container ship about 1972. She had a primitive Collision Avoidance Radar and a bridge tape recorder, a "black box" like those in airplane cockpits. For some reason, it never worked. The ship had a bridge-controlled engine room, but union work rules prohibited the mates from touching the controls. Round trips to the Mediterranean were seventy-five days, outbound with profitable cargoes for North Atlantic Treaty Organization bases and back with containers.

AEL was bought by the family-run Farrell Lines in 1978. I made one more trip to India on the *SS Export Buyer.* Farrell had about thirteen ships in the African trades and no experience in India or the Far East, but replaced AEL's agents with Farrell people. Generations of Indian families had been AEL agents. The new Farrell agents lost business because they did not know AEL's trade and did not have the necessary connections to obtain cargoes. By 1981, Farrell was on its way down to running four old ships to the Mediterranean. Liner companies were seeing the end of business, as they knew it.

Mr. Bullock:

My only experience with liner service was as Second Mate on Crowley Maritime's *MV Ambassador* about 1992. She was German-built, 22,000 tons, 650 feet long, and made fifteen-day round trips from Miami to Panama and Costa Rica with forty-foot containers. While I was aboard, *Ambassador* continually lost the plant, would then roll in the seas, and lose containers overboard.

PASSENGER LINERS

Commodore Alexanderson:

After I got married in 1934, my objective was to get into passenger ships to avoid the long India and around-the-world voyages. A friend of my older brother worked at United States Lines (USL) and arranged an interview for me with the Marine Superintendent, Captain Schuyler Cummings.

I was assigned as Third Mate in the SS California, owned by Panama Pacific Line, part of International Mercantile Marine, an American-owned consortium. She had been built in 1927, 30,260 tons, and 601 feet long. With 13,500 horsepower turbo electric twin-screw propulsion, the California was capable of 18 knots. The ship arrived in New York on Monday and sailed on the following Saturday with 600 passengers for Cuba, where cargo was discharged and loaded. After an 8 A.M. transit of the Panama Canal, in Balboa we discharged cargo, loaded bananas, and sailed at 11 P.M. for San Pedro and San Francisco. My first trip was scheduled for thirty-five days, but, due to the 1936 maritime strike, lasted three and a half months. The passengers got off in San Pedro and went home however they could.

About 1938 the California and her sister ships, Pennsylvania and Virginia, were sold to Moore McCormack Lines to become part of President Roosevelt's Good Neighbor Fleets to build trade between the U.S. and South America. Mooremac had previously been in the Scandinavian trade and took over the east coast of South America trade from the four-ship Munson Line. I was loaned to Mooremac as First Officer in the renamed California, the SS Uruguay. In my job as the Cargo Officer, when we arrived in New York, I changed from my uniform into old clothes and went into the ship's holds.

After a voyage as Senior Second Officer on USL's *President Roosevelt*, I went into the flagship, the *SS Manhattan*. Two mates, a Second Mate and a Third Mate, stood each watch in the passenger ships.

The *Manhattan*, built about 1933, ran from New York to Cobh, Ireland; Le Havre, France; Hamburg, Germany; and Southampton, England. When the war started in Europe in 1939, we made several fast trips to New York with refugees. They even slept on cots in the ship's lounges.

Because my seniority with USL continued while I was in the Navy, I went as Staff Captain in the *SS Washington*, sister ship to the *Manhattan*, in 1946. We carried 1700 to 1800 passengers from Europe to the U.S. Many of them were war brides, so numerous babies were born at sea.

USL's *SS America*, built in 1940, had sailed in the Caribbean passenger trade under Captain Giles Stedman, later Superintendent of the U.S. Merchant Marine Academy. During World War II, she became the Troop Ship *West Point* and was returned to USL in November 1946.

When I was transferred to the *America* as Executive Officer, I expected my predecessor to brief me on my duties. His only advice, and I think the reason for his transfer, was, "Don't proposition a girl on the dance floor. It echoes all over the room."

The Captain was Commodore Harry Manning, a graduate of the New York Nautical School known as "Rescue Harry" because he participated in so many rescues at sea. He was a colorful man, who wore a mink coat over his uniform. He prohibited smoking on the bridge. Manning had been Amelia Earhart's navigator and was badly injured in a plane crash with her in Hawaii. During Manning's year of recuperation, she found another navigator, who disappeared with her in the Pacific.

The *America* was advertised at twenty-four knots, but did about twenty-two. I spent four years crossing the Atlantic in her without a vacation.

In 1953, I returned to the *America* as Executive Officer and Relief Master, relieving Dick Patterson, a 1923 New York Nautical School graduate, who became the first Naval Reserve Rear Admiral at USL. A couple of voyages later, when I was relieving as Master for the first time, fog was coming in prior to our usual 4 P.M. sailing. I decided to sail anyway. As we got into the Hudson River, it completely closed in, and I felt my great responsibility. Thanks to all our navigational equipment, we made a safe passage through New York Harbor.

I was assigned to the *SS United States* as Executive Officer in September 1955 and remained in her fourteen years. I don't know how many voyages I made. She'd been operating for three years when I joined her, I had some vacation time, and I laid her up on Voyage Number 400.

The *United States*, 53,300 tons, 990 feet long, 101 feet wide, quadruple-screw, was built for USL at Newport News Shipbuilding and Dry Dock Company, Newport News, Virginia at an approximate cost of $70,000,000. She set an eastbound speed record of three days, ten hours, forty-two minutes at an average speed of thirty-five knots on her maiden voyage on July 3, 1952. Returning she set a westbound record of three days, twelve hours, twelve minutes at an average speed of thirty-five and a half knots.

Commodore Harry Manning made her first two trips, came ashore with USL, and was replaced by Commodore John W. Anderson, a 1915 graduate of the New York Nautical School. I relieved Anderson for his vacation forty four times before succeeding him as Master in February 1964. All three Masters of the *United States* graduated from the New York Nautical School.

I had an excellent crew of 1,040, many with non-seagoing jobs, like the musicians in Myer Davis' seventeen-piece orchestra, the operators of the three beauty shops, three gift shops, and two theaters, as well as the big Galley Department.

We figured four days and eight hours at thirty-two knots from New York to Le Havre. To reduce fuel consumption, we ran on six boilers, not the eight used to set the speed records. Scheduling was tight - sail from New York at noon, arrive off Le Havre Lightship at 5 A.M., dock at 6 A.M., meet the boat train, and sail at 9:30 A.M. for Southampton.

After docking at Southampton at 3 P.M., we'd lay over until noon the next day, return to Le Havre for 6 P.M. docking, discharge cargo, and sail for New York at 11 P.M.

Four days and eight hours later, we arrived Ambrose Lightship at 5 A.M. At 6:15 A.M. off Staten Island, U.S. Customs and Immigration and USL's Paymaster came aboard. We were off the pier at 7:15 A.M. and docked by 8 A.M. The gangways were not in place until 8:05 A.M. because the stevedores got five minutes to walk down the pier.

If we lost any time due to bad weather and couldn't dock by 10 A.M., we aimed for a 1 P.M. docking or, if not docking by 3 P.M., a 7 P.M. docking. It was important to avoid docking during the "golden hours," mealtimes, when the stevedores were paid at double time.

As Master of the *United States* I was also Commodore of USL's fleet. For this I was paid an extra $50 a month, but in the 1960s, my annual salary never exceeded $24,000.

The *United States* was rated for 1956 passengers, but I never carried more than 1750. My favorite passengers were businessmen who made three or four trips a year with their wives. The Duke and Duchess of Windsor often took a suite. President and Mrs. Harry Truman came to the bridge at 6:30 A.M. arriving New York to thank me for a pleasant voyage. Their daughter Margaret was a frequent passenger. President and Mrs. Dwight D. Eisenhower wrote me a very nice thank-you letter after a voyage. Prince Ranier of Monaco was a delightful person. He went westbound when he was courting Grace Kelly. Both of them later traveled to the U.S. with me for the birth of their first daughter. I also carried Princess Grace's father and her brother John's racing shell to England and France. John Wayne signed his letters to me "Duke." Senator and Mrs. John F. Kennedy were aboard. Aristotle Onassis never sailed with me, but paid a pleasant visit to the ship and spoke Greek with my Steward, Pete.

By 1961, large airplanes were taking our transatlantic passengers. We added Caribbean cruises and once a thirty-nine-day cruise to Curacao, Netherlands Antilles; Rio de Janeiro, Capetown, and Port Elizabeth, South Africa; Luanda, Angola; the Canary Islands, and Madeira.

The author was a Third Mate on American Export Lines' *SS Constitution*, in 1963. Built in 1950, and sister ship to the *SS Independence,* she was 30,000 tons, 683 feet long, and carried up to 1088 passengers in New York to the Mediterranean service. Both ships were laid-up in 1967. American Hawaii Cruises began operating them under the U.S. flag in 1978. While under tow to a Far East scrap yard in November 1997, the *Constitution* sank in a Pacific storm.

TANKERS

Captain Atkinson:

From September 1935 until July 1936, I was AB and later Bosun, on the SS *Sylvan Arrow*, a 7797 gross-ton tanker specially built for the case oil trade to China. Cases of two five-gallon tins each could be stowed in the tween deck above the tanks. Cargo booms fitted at each of the eight hatches made her look more like a cargo ship than a tanker. While I was aboard, we carried bulk oil from Beaumont, Texas to Staten Island, New York for Socony Vacuum.

In the early-1950s, I spent a year and a half as Master of the SS *Mandoil*, a Liberty Tanker of 7243 gross tons, carrying crude oil from Aruba to Scotland.

In October, 1959, I was assigned as Chief Mate to the Steam Tanker (ST) *National Defender* under construction at Newport News Shipbuilding and Dry Dock Company for operation by National Shipping and Trading Corporation. She was 810 feet long with a beam of 104 feet to allow transit of the Panama Canal, and had the largest loaded displacement of any U.S. tanker, 82,678 tons. On launching she cost $19,000,000. I took her out as Master on her maiden voyage on March 16, 1960, and commanded her until she was sold to Isbrandtsen in 1966. We mainly carried oil from Ras Tanura, Saudi Arabia to Japan.

On January 26, 1961, the Greek Royal Family and members of the government visited us in Piraeus, Greece, a unique event for the U.S. Merchant Marine.

In 1968, I returned to the *National Defender* as Relief Master for Isbrandtsen, doing U.S. Military Sea Transportation Service charters.

In 1969, I was Relief Master on the SS *Western Clipper*, an 18,000-ton tanker built for long-term charters to the U.S. Navy. My letter of April 2, 1969, from Subic Bay in the Philippines to the Port Captain shows the tanker Master's job: "....I was disappointed with our poor lifting this voyage, but it could not be helped. There was a shortage of Navy special (fuel) at Ras Tanura, and the loading rate was very slow. As we were at South Pier we had to leave on high water, but we continued loading to the limit of safety, sailing about 400 tons short of the tonnage I had intended.

As a matter of record, I do not like the arrangement of using no. 10 wings as bunker tanks. As the fuel is consumed, the ship trims by the head and the sagging stress is greatly increased, especially when cargo must be moved from forward to amidships to bring the head up. Also, I dislike the heavy rolling, but that is the fault of the designers, as I have no doubt you are fully aware.... ...small quantities of stores may be picked up off Singapore without entering the port and while under way, unless the laws have changed lately. I did this several times with the *Defender* a few years ago...."

My next letter was dated April 16, 1969, from Bahrain: "We had an uneventful passage from Subic, arriving here well ahead of original ETA despite adverse winds the last couple of days. We started loading at noon today and expect to sail about 0900 tomorrow. I assume you have seen the notation on the Subic discharge report re five hours for hookup at the Monobuoy. I find this sort of thing very annoying, probably because there is nothing I can do about it. We reduced speed to arrive at the pilot station at 0500 the 2 nd, pilot and tugs being available at that time, a loss to us of about five hours...samples are taken and run through the lab before discharging commences...after discharge, we had to wait over two hours beyond our posted and agreed upon sailing time for the pilot and tug to come to us.

....mail service seems very poor lately, not much at Subic and nothing at all here excepting mail addressed directly to the agent. Will you see if you can speed up our mail deliveries, please? It would eliminate a lot of discontent...."

Excess stability built into the *Western Clipper* caused her to roll excessively, even at the dock. I'm a fair weather sailor and like things smooth, so I got off after seven months. My older son and his friend, Rock, were on her as Ordinary Seamen. We three paid off in Rota, Spain, drove to Paris, and flew to London to meet Rock's parents. My son was on ships since he was three months old and at age nine, went around the world with his mother and me. On a trip to India when my son was thirteen, the Chief Mate told me that he was the best worker he ever had. I promoted him to Acting AB on the *Western Clipper*.

In 1969, I went on the *ST Western Hunter*, similar to the *National Defender*, but a knot slower. We carried oil from Mina al Ahmadi, Kuwait to Cagliari, Sardinia and Portland, Maine, oil from Tobruk, Libya to St. Croix, Virgin Islands, and grain from Houston to Sandheads, India.

I was again Relief Master on the *National Defender* in 1970 and 1971, and back on the *Western Hunter* from 1971-1973.

On August 31, 1973, I took my last Master's job, on the *SS Overseas Arctic* of Maritime Overseas Corporation. She was a 34,440- gross ton stem winder, everything aft with no forward house. I stayed on her, picking up Nigerian oil, until January 23 1974. This job told me that the oil shortage in the U.S. was phony. We brought full cargoes to Marcus Hook, Pennsylvania to top off oil tanks there and later had to wait three days for a berth in St. Croix to discharge.

Captain Schindler:

My second trip as a Third Mate, on Keystone Shipping Company's *SS Key Trader* in 1962, running coastwise with multiple clean products, such as gasoline and kerosene, began my career in tankers.

Next I made a "pier head jump," the term for being ready at the MM&P Hall when a company calls in an immediate opening, onto the *SS Mission Buenaventura*, a 10,650-ton T-2 tanker.

I was on watch departing Melville, Rhode Island at night. The Captain, who I later learned drank excessively and didn't spend a lot of time on the bridge, said, "It's all yours." I asked our destination, and he told me Curacao. I'd never heard of it and asked what course to steer. He replied, "Whatever course is necessary." Only four months out of school, I followed the last course on the chart. Curacao, Netherlands Antilles was at the end of the penciled line.

A week later, three miles from the Curacao Pilot Station, I called the Captain. He asked if the Pilot was aboard yet. When I said no, the Captain did not come to the bridge. I stopped the engines, boarded the Pilot and again called the Captain, who asked if we were docked yet.

We loaded Number 6 Bunker C, a crude heavy oil, for U.S. Navy ships and discharged it at Tampa, Key West, and Jacksonville, Florida and Norfolk.

I would have stayed longer on this ship, but I missed it in Tampa. I asked the Port Engineer how long we would be in the shipyard. He told me another week, so I went to the dog track in St. Petersburg. When I returned the ship was gone, and my bags were at the agent's office. I made my own way to Philadelphia, collected my wages from Keystone, and registered at the MM&P Hall in Providence, Rhode Island.

In 1964, I moved to Houston, Texas because shipping was better there. Also, I had decided that I was a tankerman because I could handle the loading and discharging myself instead of dealing with problems caused by stevedores. For example, a Captain once sent me into a hold to tell the longshoremen to stop pilfering the cargo, and one of them pulled a knife on me.

After a relief trip as Third Mate on the *SS Key Trader*, running coastwise with clean oil, I got my first permanent job through a pier head jump in Melville, Rhode Island. The *SS Henry*, built in 1938, was a prototype of the World War II T-2 tanker with an electric motor. I was Third Mate for a week, Second Mate for a year and Chief Mate for five years.

We ran Navy black oil from Curacao to Key West, Jacksonville and Melville. Then we cleaned the ship for the grain trade, taking wheat, sorghum, and milo from Port Arthur, Texas to Bombay via the Suez Canal. The trips took three months - one month over, a month discharging, and a month coming back.

Sometimes we only swept the tanks after discharging the grain and proceeded to Kuwait for oil. Thorough cleaning of the tanks was done by Butterworthing, named for the most common system. Two or three nozzles rotate in a vertical plane, while the body of the machine rotates in a horizontal plane, spraying 110 gallons of sea water at 150 pounds of pressure per minute on the walls of the tank for an hour at ten, twenty, and thirty-foot levels. Cold water was pumped into the tanks continuously for a week to a month to remove the crude oil residue, followed by ventilation with blowers and hand mucking up the scale into buckets. Pollution controls now require that the residue be pumped into a holding tank, which reduces the ship's cargo capacity.

In the late-1960s, I spent my longest stretch at sea, forty-two days, on the *SS Sabine*, a T-2 elongated from 500 to 600 feet, with oil from Ras-el-Tinnurah, Saudi Arabia via the Cape of Good Hope to Halifax, Nova Scotia. The heat in these oil-loading ports was intense. The 8 A.M. temperature at Mina al Ahmadi, Kuwait was 120 degrees, and the noon temperature was above the range of the thermometer. A week of loading meant feet burning on the deck, heat rash, and diarrhea.

In 1970, at age thirty, I got my first Master's job. The *SS Atlantic* was a 50,000-tonner, just sold to operate under the Liberian flag and awaiting her permanent Indian Captain. We loaded oil at Kharg Island, Iran for Israel. The official destination, for the benefit of both parties to the charter, was "Aden for orders." In the Straits of Hormuz the Indian Bosun accidentally chopped his toe off. I tried without success to stitch it and had to put him off at Kharg Island.

In the early-1970s, I became Master of the *SS Rambam*, 18,000 tons, owned and operated by American Bulk Carriers under the U.S. flag. Originally a tanker, she carried bulk cargoes, mostly grain to India. She was the ugliest ship I ever saw because part of the midship house had been moved aft over the shelter deck. Her Jewish owner arrived at the name as a contraction of the philosophy and great works of the Egyptian Jewish philosopher Moses Miamonades.

On my next ship, the *SS Spitfire*, after loading grain in New Orleans, I learned that 1200 tons of ballast could not be pumped out, meaning that we were one foot overloaded. I sailed the ship. By listing the ship offshore, the Plimsoll mark was acceptable to the Panama Canal Pilot on boarding. Entering the canal, the marks indicated overloaded, but we were in fresh water, so all right. Bunkering in Honolulu added to our overload. Fortunately, a swell running in the harbor made it difficult for the Coast Guard officer to read our marks. He suggested that they be repainted up higher, where they could be read.

Spitfire was a geared bulk carrier, that is, had booms for discharging grain. We used them at Inchon, Korea.

During the 1973 oil shortage in the U.S., we had 150,000 barrels of Number 2 heating oil aboard and made four ports on the East Coast trying to discharge it. The storage facilities were already full. Finally, we discharged parts of it in Boston, Charleston, and Wilmington, Delaware. I had a similar experience on the *SS Mount Hope* with oil loaded in Puerto Rico.

After American Bulk Carriers went out of business, I got a Master's job with Hudson Waterways on the 26,000-

ton tanker *SS Transpanama* about 1974. We carried oil and then grain to the Soviet Union. In the Black Sea ports of Il'ichevsk and Poti they fumigated the cargo to clean out weevils. This required shutting down the power plant and staying in a rotten hotel for two or three days. A large Soviet inspection party claimed to have found weevils in three tanks. I asked to see samples from each tank. After numerous conferences, they produced one dead weevil. I insisted on seeing a live weevil, which they could not find. Mine was the only ship taking grain to the Black Sea not fumigated. Discharging the grain into trains took six weeks because we had to wait up to a week between trains.

I lost my job on the *Transpanama* because while I was on vacation, another Master sunk his ship and was given mine due to his seniority with the company.

My job as Master of the *SS Galaxy*, in dead ship status in Antigua, British West Indies, was to clean her tanks so she would not burn during scrapping. The owner had entered her into an unprofitable sub-charter arrangement, so was scrapping the ship to save money. She was towed to Spain, where we spent another month cleaning her before scrapping.

In 1977, I was Chief Mate on the *SS American Hawk*. She and the *American Eagle* were the two T-2 tankers owned by American Foreign Steamship Company, a good company. Their tanks were coated with Demetcoat, a Teflon-like coating to which oil does not adhere, as it does to steel. Application of it requires sand-blasting of residual oil. Most ships now have it.

During this period, Chief Mates earned about $13,000 a month, more than Masters, by working six hours on and six hours off and frequently around the clock. Once, we entered Norfolk on a Wednesday. There was a strike at the dock, so we had to discharge our oil into barges. I took only naps between barges. On departure the following Tuesday, as Chief Mate I had to stand by the anchor. I did not sleep in a bed, have a hot meal, or shower in those seven days, but was paid plenty in overtime.

From 1979-1984, I was Master of my last ship, the U.S. Naval Ship (USNS) *Hudson*, built about 1974, 37,267 tons, 720 feet long, twin diesel with automated engine room and cargo system. The *Hudson* could not successfully operate commercially because of design flaws in her automated cargo system. The Military Sealift Command took her under long-term charter to carry fuel to Navy depots worldwide, out-of-the-way places like Ascension Island in the South Atlantic. We carried five grades of clean products, including highly explosive JP (Jet Propulsion) 4 and JP 5 fuel. With stern hoses we refueled destroyers at sea. My first trip went around the world. The paperwork was staggering until I learned the Navy's methods.

Captain Smeenk:

By 1974, I had been working and vacationing out of the U.S. for so long that I had no MM&P shipping card. I had not presented myself once a month at the MM&P Hall in the port I wanted to sail out of. To work I had to sail on my only oil tanker, Second Mate on the USNS *Yukon*, a 30,000-ton tanker, for the Military Sealift Command.

We carried 250,000 barrels of jet fuel to U.S. military bases in Puerto Rico, Scotland and Iceland. Steaming into the fjord in Iceland, I realized that our destination was the World War II fueling base that my father, a U.S. Navy Seabee, had helped build.

In collision avoidance situations I was used to the quick response of freighters. I found the inertia of a fully loaded tanker three times the displacement of a freighter surprising and had to react faster.

Captain Sulzer:

About 1976, I spent a year on the *SS Exxon Baltimore*, 50,000 tons, and the *Exxon Washington*, both split house tankers, one midships and one aft, running coastwise with refined products. Here I learned a lesson about seamen. I asked one of them to watch a ballast tank being filled with water. He went off for a smoke and let the tank overflow.

In the summer of 1979, I was on Getty Oil's *SS Delaware City*, a 650-foot, tramp T-5 product tanker of about 28,000 tons. The loading port was different on each voyage - Venezuela, St. Croix and St. Thomas in the Virgin Islands, and San Juan, Puerto Rico. One of my jobs as Junior Third Mate was copying the rough log into the smooth log. This nightly practice continued long after the introduction of carbon paper. Getty went out of business about a year later.

Ms. Preston:

With Exxon I went to the specialty tankers, called drugstore ships. They carried fifteen to thirty one grades of products, such as rubbing alcohol, wax and caustic soda. The *SS Exxon Huntington*, 28,000 tons, and *Exxon Gettysburg*, 40,000 tons, were built in the late-1950s. Over the years, pumps and lines were added, making a mishmash of centrifugal, reciprocating and deep-well pumps on these tankers.

To be able to get home quickly in an emergency, in 1983 I went on the *SS Exxon Galveston*, a 40,000-ton lighter constructed by welding a tug into the stern of an ocean going barge. Tankers bringing crude oil from the North Slope of Alaska to San Francisco were loaded too deeply to reach the dock, so the *Galveston* discharged them out in the harbor. Many of the crewmembers lived in San Francisco and rotated home every seven days. After almost a year on her, I wanted a ship where everyone was away from their families, not just myself.

I made only one trip to Alaska, as Second Mate on the *SS Exxon New Orleans*. My husband sailed in the Alaska trade for eight of his eleven years with Exxon.

In 1985, I made my first trip as Chief Mate, on the *SS Exxon Baltimore*, sister to my first ship, the *SS Exxon Boston*. She had been a processing ship, capturing vapors emitted in transferring product from crude oil platforms about five miles off Santa Barbara, California. Loading was completely closed to prevent vapors entering the atmosphere. Reconverted to a regular tanker, she did a triangular run - down to Chiriqui Grande, Panama, a lovely cove and the eastern end of the Trans-Panama Pipeline, to load crude oil, and discharge it at Bayway, New Jersey. After flushing the crude from the lines and tanks with heating oil, the tanks were heated with steam that was superheated to 280-290 degrees, and asphalt at 325-350 degrees was loaded.

The asphalt flowed on very slowly over thirty six to forty hours. After discharge at Baton Rouge, Louisiana the tanks were flushed again to prevent the asphalt residue from solidifying.

As Chief Mate on a tanker the pre-loading plan was my responsibility. The sequence of products is critical. The best grade must go in first and the worst grade last. The Mate is on deck for the start of loading and relies on the Second or Third Mate to check the ullages, the space left in the tanks. Since 1981-1982, tankers have closed loading. Ullages are checked by gauges, not by opening the tanks and looking into them. I learned the old system and found it difficult to rely on gauges and not look into the tanks. However, I was gassed while loading gasoline on a hot Texas day. The vapors were visibly thick as I looked into a tank being filled. I almost passed out.

The Chief Mate is on deck for the start of the discharge operation, working with the independent inspectors to verify that the product is clean enough to be pumped ashore. The other mates check the rates of discharge to verify that the pumps are working correctly. The Chief Mate is out again for stripping, the process of cleaning out the tanks.

Where the Chief Mate really earns his money is in tank cleaning. If the ship has no automatic cleaning system, the Mate arranges the washing machines. Cleaning a ship takes at least thirty-six hours, depending on the amount of residue left by the various products. Even as we approach the 21st century, crewmembers still muck the bottoms of the tanks with little aluminum scrapers and rubber buckets, designed to avoid creating a spark. The better the cleaning job, the more cargo that can be carried by the ship.

Exxon has not paid overtime since 1982. A year earlier they redistributed workloads. The Third Mate got some of the Chief Mate's paperwork and the storing duties of the Chief Steward, who is no longer carried. The Second Mate does certain safety equipment work in addition to his chart work. Salaries are based on working twelve hours a day.

Mr. Bullock:

In December 1988, I joined the Motor Vessel *Lawrence Gianella* as Third Mate. She was a 30,000-ton, 615-foot long, T-5 tanker built in 1985, and hauled clean products at thirteen and a half knots wherever the Military Sealift Command sent us.

Half our load of JP 4 and JP 5 fuel was discharged in the Philippines and half in Japan. I learned cargo operations by reading the manuals and following the Chief Mate, who was always aboard. We then took a half-load of oil from Bahrain to Scotland, returned to Port Arthur, Texas, loaded, and carried product to the East Coast of the U.S.

The *Gianella* has a bridge-controlled, computer-monitored, diesel engine room. Members of the Engine Department work days only.

I rejoined the *Gianella* as Third Mate in 1989, with the promise that I would relieve the Second Mate, but that didn't happen.

On the SS *Gus W. Darnell*, sister ship to the *Gianella*, for six months in 1991, I learned that I don't want to be Chief Mate on a tanker. The only term for the job is run ragged as we carried oil from Singapore to Bahrain, Kuwait, and Jubal Ali in the United Arab Emirates. In 1992

I went back on the *Darnell*, tramping worldwide under charter to the Military Sealift Command, to Tule, Greenland, Scotland, Italy, Greece, Korea, Japan, and Antarctica.

TRAMPING

Captain Atkinson:

From 1954-1956, I was Master of the Liberty Ship *National Mariner*, tramping for cargoes, usually ore or grain. During loading of a full cargo of scrap iron in Montreal, Quebec, and Seven Isles, I sent the ship's compasses, chronometers, and clocks ashore to protect them from the effects of the magnets used to load the iron. She had a radar and gyrocompass, unusual for a Liberty Ship. Due to overcast on the voyage to Gijon and Bilbao, Spain, no sights were possible. I used dead reckoning and steered by the gyrocompass. Halfway across the Atlantic, the gyrocompass started giving me trouble. The magnetic compasses were unreliable because the entire ship and cargo were magnetized. I even climbed the mast trying to find a place where a magnetic compass could be used. I had a very good Second Mate, Charles Barrett, who relieved me as Master a few years later. He and I stood watch over the gyrocompass until we picked up the coast of Spain on radar. I shut down the gyrocompass and had the helmsman steer for landmarks in the old-fashioned way. By radio, I determined that there was no gyro repairman in all of Spain. After discharge in Gijon, I steered by landmarks to Bilbao.

Here the Second Mate tore down the gyro and found one little piece was cracked. He fabricated a new part, and the gyro worked perfectly.

From Bilbao we sailed way up the Orinoco River in Venezuela for a load of ore and carried it to the Delaware River. The compass adjuster who came aboard, thought that the magnetic compass in the wheelhouse was broken. I explained that we had carried a cargo of scrap iron. He corrected the compass with the largest number of magnets I ever saw. Several years later, I was aboard the *National Mariner*, when she was lightering grain in Suez under the

Liberian flag. About a third of the magnets were still attached to the compass. Without the gyrocompass on the voyage to Spain, I would have had to radio for help.

Captain Fowler:

On my first voyage as Master of American Foreign's Liberty Ship *John P. Poe* we loaded coal at Philadelphia in December, 1946, and discharged it at Rio de Janiero. From there we were sent to La Romana at the eastern end of the Dominican Republic, for a half load of sugar and then up the coast to San Pedro de Macoris to finish loading. That cargo was discharged at Liverpool. We returned to Norfolk, where I was relieved.

In September 1947, I took command of the Liberty Ship *Casimir Pulaski*, loading a full cargo of coal at Baltimore for Brindisi, Italy. At Brindisi I received orders to take on sufficient bunkers at Bari, Italy to proceed in ballast to a Black Sea Russian port to load a cargo of ore and take on bunkers again at Gibraltar or Ceuta, Morocco. By the time I cleared the Bosporus Straits, no loading port had been designated. I headed due east at slow speed. I was beginning to think that, like the Flying Dutchman of old, I would be condemned to sail the Black Sea forever, when I received a message to proceed to a point fifteen miles off Novorossiysk, where a pilot would meet us. Before daylight, we picked up the lighthouse off to port, and just a little later, thick fog set in. I headed up the coast at dead speed, far enough off it I hoped. At noon, I reversed course and headed back down the coast. About 2:00 P.M., the weather cleared, and we picked up the pilot.

After we docked, a party of Soviets kept the crew in the mess rooms while searching the ship. They were mainly interested in American magazines.

Another American Foreign ship, the *SS Peter Desmet*, was in the loading berth. We had to wait about a week before loading. Women did most of the work, leveling out the ore with shovels and hatch tending. They were not allowed to talk to the crewmembers. The only men I saw were guards. They had enough of them. The agent came aboard every day at 11:00 A.M., had lunch with me and then departed. I supposed that food was short. For the seventeen days we were there, I never left the ship. From what the crew told me, there wasn't much to see anyway, and the people weren't friendly. We stopped in Ceuta for bunkers and discharged the ore in Baltimore in December 1947.

In early-1948, I became Master of the Liberty Ship *Thomas R. Marshall* and made several trips to Italy with coal.

During the years after World War II, many Liberty Ships were being turned back to the government. American Foreign turned back all but the four they purchased and renamed. About 1948, I became Chief Mate on the *SS American Oriole*, formerly the *Nathan Clifford,* on a voyage from Galveston, Texas to Italy, Greece, and Turkey. After carrying a load of grain from Galveston to Germany, we loaded about 3,500 tons of general cargo at Antwerp, Belgium for New York. There was no further charter, so the crew was paid off, and the vessel was tied up in Hoboken, New Jersey.

I was home only a short time, when I received a call back to the *American Oriole*. She had obtained a charter to take a cargo of nitrate soda from Hopewell, Virginia to Yugoslavia. We loaded up to 18 feet mean draft, the deepest allowed on the James River. The balance of the cargo went in freight cars to Norfolk, where we loaded to our marks and sailed. This voyage was to last about forty days, but turned out to be the longest I was away from home with the exception of World War II.

After discharging, the Captain was ordered to proceed to San Francisco, and told that further orders would be given as we went through the Panama Canal. The ship was chartered to the Military Sea Transportation Service, and we were ordered to Seattle. There the Master was transferred to the *SS American Eagle*, and I became Master.

We were fitted out with pad eyes on the decks, chains, and turnbuckles for deck loads of lumber. At Aberdeen, Washington we took on a full cargo of lumber for Pearl Harbor.

After discharging, we loaded crated boxes for San Diego.

From San Diego we proceeded up the coast, took on some lumber in Coos Bay, Oregon and finished loading at Eureka, California.

By the time we arrived in Yokohama with a fairly high deck load, the ship was very becoming very tender. I requested the agent to arrange for bunkers, so that I could get some weight in my double bottoms. Otherwise, it would have been necessary to ballast my tanks with salt water. A small tanker met us at the anchorage with bunkers. At the agent's office I learned that our cargo was to be discharged at Nagoya, Japan.

After discharge at Nagoya, we were ordered back to Yokohama. I waited two weeks at anchor before docking to take on Army cargo for the Oakland, California Army Base.

While laying at the dock at Oakland for about a month, I called the agent every day at 4 P.M., for orders. Finally, he told me that the ship had come off military charter, and a new charter had been obtained.

I was ordered to proceed the next day, to Portland, Oregon where we loaded a full cargo of grain for La Spezia, Italy. On my last day in La Spezia, the owners informed me that the ship had been chartered to the Alcoa Steamship Company, and I should proceed to Paramaribo, Dutch Guyana for a cargo of bauxite. We loaded to a mean depth of 16 feet, the deepest you could take over the bar at the entrance of the river. Small feeder vessels ran bauxite from Paramaribo to Trinidad. We topped off at Trinidad and proceeded to Baton Rouge, Louisiana.

I had been on the ship for about a year without going home, so I called American Foreign for a relief. The Port Captain told me that the vessel was already under orders to return to Paramaribo in ballast for another cargo. I made the next voyage and was relieved in New Orleans.

After two weeks at home, I relieved the sick Master of the half-loaded *SS American Starling.* When loading of Army cargo was completed, we proceeded to the eastern most island in the Azores chain, a small place where we laid at anchor to discharge, and then proceeded to Casablanca.

Captain White:

About 1950, grain shipments increased. I drove to Galveston with a friend and took a Second Mate's job on the *SS Skystar*, a Liberty ship bound for Trieste. When I went aboard, she felt familiar. I saw the bunk that I had the Carpenter build in the corner of the wheelhouse in Okinawa and my name on the charts. The Captain verified that she had been the *SS Frank Adair Monroe*, the ship I had commanded in the South Pacific during World War II. It was a pleasant round trip.

Mr. Ramsey:

In the late-1970s, I went on the *SS Flora*, an old Bethlehem Steel ore carrier, for a couple of trips between Tampa and Stockton, California. She was a wreck and had sunk about three times hauling steel.

About 1986, Apex Marine built ships in Korea. I got a relief Third Mate's job on the *MV Altair*, a 38,000-ton bulk carrier with seven holds for grain, bulk ore, chemicals and phosphate, on her maiden voyage from Seattle. By this time, I had moved from Maine to the San Francisco area.

I made trips on the *Altair* and the *MV Aspen* to the Third World. Liberty Maritime was spun off Apex Marine, and all the ships were renamed *Liberty*, like *Liberty Spirit,*

69

the former *Altair*. A typical trip was winter wheat from Portland, Oregon to Chittagong, Bangladesh and return to New Orleans for grain.

Captain Smeenk:

In the absence of return cargoes in the early-1970s, Isthmian relied on military cargoes to Vietnam and U.S. Agency for International Development (AID) shipments of wheat and foodstuffs to India. U.S. law dictates that a certain percentage of AID cargoes move in U.S. ships. Old ships carried AID cargoes, which the consignees had to accept, but returned empty because shippers would not use them.

About 1972, after discharging wheat in India, we proceeded to Taiwan, where we loaded AID fertilizer for Surabaja, Indonesia. As Chief Mate, I ordered rough cleaning of the holds because the charterer had allowed only $250 for cleaning. By the time we returned to Houston, wheat had sprouted in the fertilizer residue and had to be cleaned out at the U.S. labor rate of $250 per hour per hold.

Mr. Bullock:

In July 1989, I was Third Mate on Ogden Marine's *SS OMI Missouri*, built about 1980, 700 feet long and 20,000 tons, taking corn from Portland, Oregon to Pondicherry on the east coast of India. Making eleven - twelve knots against a steady southwest wind, the trip took 39 days. Along the coast of Malaysia I saw pirates in unlighted powerful tugs and fishing boats. To discourage any attempts to board us, we turned on all the deck lights and had patrols on deck with fire hoses.

Using huge bucket cranes, discharge from our five hatches into three small vessels took seven days.

We returned in ballast via the Suez Canal, and beat Hurricane Hugo to Norfolk, Virginia by two days.

SPECIALIZED SHIPS

Admiral Bauman:

Through my Massachusetts Maritime Academy classmate John Gibbons, in August 1948 I became what was known as "a coal boat stiff." Pocahontas Fuel Company's *SS James Elwood Jones* was built in 1916, 365 feet long, 3,500 - 4,000 tons, a small tanker with hatches for loading 6,000 tons of coal at Norfolk, Virginia. There were then about thirty five to forty coal boats running on the East Coast, nine owned by Pocahontas, fifteen by Mystic and the rest by Sprague and Berwin Fuel Company.

Hospital Point Lighthouse, leaving Salem, Massachusetts, is the lower end of the navigational range at the entrance to the Cape Cod Canal. At this point the Captain would order, "Steer southwest by south one quarter south." Out of habit the coal boats were steered by magnetic compass only, not using degrees for headings.

I was the only member of the crew who did not live at the Virginia end of the two and half-day voyage, so I remained on board to supervise the loading, and everyone else went home.

On arrival off Norfolk, one captain blew the ship's whistle like a calliope. At home his dog barked, signaling the Captain's wife to pick him up at the dock. The Captain kissed his dog, shook hands with his wife, and drove off.

Ten minutes before departure, I had to blow the steam whistle on the ship's fifty-foot-high stack to call the crew back. If I blew it too early, woe to me on the northbound leg of the voyage.

During loading, coal dust was everywhere. I took to buying used coveralls, wearing them with the collar and cuffs taped closed, and throwing the suit overboard on departure.

Discharge ports for our coal varied - Providence, Rhode Island; New Bedford, Boston, and Salem,

Massachusetts; Portsmouth, New Hampshire; Portland and Searsport, Maine. I have a second page on my Master's license listing the New England ports where I'm qualified to act as a pilot. Because I always stayed aboard in Virginia, I was off in New England. My family moved to New Bedford so we could spend a couple of days together on each trip.

Captain Glen:

President Eisenhower conceived the Nuclear Ship *Savannah* in 1955, as part of the Atoms for Peace Program. Her mission was waving the U.S. flag around the world for the peaceful use of atomic energy. The *Savannah*, 22,00 tons, 595 feet long with a beam of 78 feet, was launched in 1959. States Marine Lines was the operator, but she was struck for a year over manning problems between the MM&P and the Marine Engineers Beneficial Association (MEBA). In 1963, the U.S. Government gave her to First Atomic Transport, a wholly owned subsidiary of American Export Lines. I joined her in the mid-1960s, as a Deck Trainee. Within a couple of months, I was Third Officer.

The *Savannah* was a joint project of the Federal Maritime Administration and the U.S. Atomic Energy Commission (AEC), now the U.S. Nuclear Regulatory Commission. After a year of shipboard and Maritime Administration training at the U.S. Merchant Marine Academy and passing an AEC examination, I got my Nuclear Reactor Operator's license.

Although *Savannah* carried general cargo, our jobs were also to be ambassadors so that people would get used to an atomic-powered ship using their ports. Before a port call an advance team met with the port authority to write a procedure. We made ports in Northern Europe, Spain, Italy, France, Greece, Hong Kong, Taiwan, Korea, and Manila. The Japanese claimed that insurance regulations wouldn't permit us to call in Japan, but I believe that their decision was political.

I participated in the first refueling of the *Savannah's* nuclear reactor, at the Nuclear Division of Todd Shipyard in Galveston, Texas. My assignment, as Health Physics Technician, was to control radiation and protect the crew working in the reactor spaces and surrounding areas. On the *Savannah* everything was done right, with no compromises of safety and integrity.

The *Savannah* had the latest cargo handling equipment, but was not a working cargo ship. She looked sleek due to her raked masts and absence of jumbo booms. The crew was larger than that of a regular cargo ship - with nineteen licensed engineers, four to a watch, and a large Steward's Department to serve the sixty passengers *Savannah* could carry. We never carried passengers, except for some dignitaries. Savannah had the most up-to-date navigation equipment. Navigating the English Channel on her, I was particularly impressed with the Decca electronic navigation system.

At the time, the thinking was that, if oil ever got to six or seven dollars a barrel, nuclear power would be the way to go. Oil then cost three dollars a barrel, so in late 1971, after a year idle in Galveston, the *Savannah* was laid-up.

I enjoyed my years as Third and Second Officer on the *Savannah*. A coffee break with the great minds in her crew was more a learning experience. I learned not to fear technology. The courses I had to take in health physics, water chemistry, and electronics were good training for the job that I do today.

By 1979, I had left American Export Lines and was living on a boat in Key Largo, Florida. One Sunday I saw an advertisement by Tracor Marine in the *Miami Herald* for a Master on a research vessel. After an interview in Port Everglades, Florida I was hired on the spot as Master of the R/V *H.J.W. Fay*, 461 gross tons, 175 feet long with a beam of 32 feet, and powered by twin-screw diesel engines rated at 2,400 horsepower.

After U.S. Navy nuclear submarines were dry-docked and overhauled at the base in Holy Loch, Scotland we would rendezvous with them at sea and make noise, so that they could recalibrate their sonars. Trips lasted four days. Otherwise, we were docked, and I enjoyed returning to my Scottish roots in nearby Dunoon, Argyle.

As Master of a 13-man crew plus Tracor's scientific staff, I got very good ship-handling experience off the coast of Scotland. I also learned the business of running a ship, what I call "forensic seamanship," keeping good records to avoid lawsuits.

After almost a year, Tracor's contract with the Navy ended. I brought the *Fay* back to Port Everglades via the Canary Islands.

About 1976, American Export Lines' company union, the Brotherhood of Marine Officers (BMO), was merging with the MEBA. In anticipation of contracts for liquefied natural gas (LNG) ships, some of us American Export Lines' deck officers received LNG training at MEBA's Calhoun School in Baltimore. However, after completing the eight-week course, I returned to their freighters.

In 1980, Energy Transportation Corporation, of New York, offered me a Third Mate's job with great prospects on their U.S. flag LNG ships. I made a couple of two-week trips as Third Mate, then as Second Mate, as Observing Chief Mate and, within a couple of months of joining them, as Chief Mate on the *LNG Aquarius*. She is the oldest of the eight LNG ships delivered between 1977 and 1980, 100,000 gross tons, 963 feet long with a beam of 142 1/2 feet, and 43,000 horsepower. Her cargo of liquefied natural gas is carried at minus 260 degrees Fahrenheit.

My success with this company has been a combination of luck and experience, being in the right place at the right time with the right qualifications. I had Master's experience and a technical background, yet was young enough to complete the ships' twenty-year contracts. It's a good company and has given me many opportunities to go to schools, like ship handling, Master Mariners Readiness

Program, fire fighting, ship's medicine, and management seminars. I got my Master's license at age thirty and was sailing on it by age thirty-six.

The ships are chartered to Burma Gas Transport a subsidiary of Burma Oil, of London. Burma Oil is the time-charterer and intermediary between the Indonesian sellers, the state-owned Ministry of Gas, and the Japanese buyers, a consortium of Japanese utility companies. The Indonesian Government operates the plant in Sumatra with Mobil Oil Corporation and the plant in Borneo with Hufco, a Texas company. There are four discharge ports in Japan, where the product is used primarily for electric generation.

Captain Sulzer:

In 1976, I returned to New York Maritime's Training Ship *Empire State V* as a watch officer on that summer's cruise to Miami, Montreal, and Operation Sail in New York City. I had been one of six First Class Cadets who helped bring her to the College from lay-up in California. My father was the Chief Engineer on that trip.

I was bored with seeing only Houston and Philadelphia on tankers, so in 1977, I spent six weeks at the MEBA's Calhoun Engineering School in Baltimore training for American Export Lines' LNG ships. The MEBA was to supply the engineers and the BMO the deck officers.

Delivery of the first of the LNG ships, *LNG Aquarius*, was delayed for almost a year. I had a choice of going back on tankers with the MEBA, but chose American Export Lines' freighters through the BMO.

By May 1980, I had I completed my Master's degree in Business Administration, and the *LNG Aquarius* was operating. I went on her as Second Mate.

Each of five one hundred-foot diameter, free-standing, aluminum spheres carried 25,000 cubic meters of LNG. *Aquarius'* 125-foot high bridge gave a twenty-two-mile line of sight. The United States was in the forefront of the design of LNG ships when *LNG Aquarius* and a sister ship were built in Quincy, Massachusetts in 1976. Three LNG ships were built in Newport News, Virginia using a membrane system of stainless steel sheets supported and insulated by the hull. They were to operate from Algeria to Cove Point on Maryland's Chesapeake Bay. Algeria raised the price, while in the U.S. natural gas prices were regulated, so the business collapsed. Avondale Shipyards in Louisiana built three LNG ships using a square freestanding design, but the insulation failed. Two of these ships were later used as bulk carriers, but the U.S. Government became the owner of eight LNG ships.

LNG Aquarius was under charter for twenty years to Burma Oil, a British company, and was operated by Energy Transportation Corporation. She loaded gas at Lhokseumawe in northeastern Sumatra and Bontang in southeastern Borneo. Discharge at Nagoya, Osaka, Heimigi, or Tobata, Japan took twenty-four hours. A Borneo round trip took ten days and a Sumatra trip fourteen. The Japanese buy natural gas to reduce their reliance on oil.

Natural gas is a product of oil fields inland and is piped to loading ports by a series of compressors, called "the train." Temperature and pressure are dropped until the gas is liquefied. The LNG is slowly pumped into tanks at the port's tank farm. It cannot explode or burn because it is not under pressure. Pumping the gas into a ship takes twelve hours. Aluminum, rather than steel, parts prevent shattering at the extreme sub-freezing temperatures. Decks are made of cement wherever they might come into contact with the gas.

The crew of twenty-eight works four months on and then gets four months off. Of the four mates, the Chief Mate works only on the cargo.

The port of Bontang, Borneo was carved from the jungle at fifteen minutes north latitude, so I've stood on the equator. At my request, the Captain once detoured so that the crew could cross the equator.

By 1982, I had a Chief Mate's license, but left Energy Transportation because, with all the officers being young, there was no advancement.

I returned to Energy Transportation in 1989, as a Third Mate, a lower rank than when I left them, because it was the best-paying job around. Laid-up ships were due to come out. The U.S. Government was selling ships that cost $200,000,000 for $20,000,000. The three membrane LNG ships were to operate from Algeria to Cove Point, Maryland for Shell Oil, and Citrus Marine was to run from Algeria to Lake Charles, Louisiana, all under U.S. flag. However, all remained in lay-up due to litigation over who would operate them.

Captain Smeenk:

In the summer of 1990, I got off Lykes' boom ships to sail as Chief Mate on the *SS Sheldon Lykes* in service from the U.S. Gulf and East Coast to the Mediterranean and Northern Europe. She was one of the first containerships built, in 1968 for the German company Hapag Lloyd, about 16,400 gross tons, 620 feet long, deck house aft, diesel-powered with a maximum speed of seventeen knots, and a capacity of 1100 twenty-foot containers.

I was Chief Mate with the first female Master of a U.S. merchant ship, Debby Dempsey, on the *SS Margaret Lykes* in the spring and summer of 1994. Captain Dempsey left Lykes in the fall of 1994, for the Columbia River Bar Pilots Association in Astoria, Oregon. Heavy north Pacific swells hitting shallow sandbars at the mouth of the Columbia River make boarding a pilot difficult. In addition to the usual navigation, the pilot has to watch that the bottom of a loaded ship does not come down hard on a sand bar and crack her hull.

Here's an example of the problems a Chief Mate encounters. In Haifa, Israel stevedores dropped one of the *Margaret Lykes* containers into the hold, puncturing a ballast tank. Ballast water mixed with bagged camomile tea loaded in Egypt, making salt-water tea. The ship listed, and a heeling pump automatically pumped water back into the tank and thus into the cargo hold. The engineers pumped the water level down and welded the damaged tank, with a delay of only five hours. These containerships carried up to twelve passengers, but I was working at least twelve hours a day and had no time to socialize.

As Chief Mate on the *SS Charlotte Lykes* in 1995, we made fifty-day round trips to the Mediterranean or thirty-day trips to Northern Europe from New York and Norfolk and occasional longer trips from the U.S. Gulf. Mediterranean ports were Livorno and Naples, Italy; Izmur, Turkey; Alexandria, Egypt, and Haifa. On Northern European voyages the *Charlotte Lykes* called at Antwerp, Bremerhaven, LeHavre, and Felixstowe, on the coast north of the River Thames and the harbor for Harwich. Maximum port time was sixteen hours for full discharge and loading, usually with three shoreside cranes. The standard measure of speed is the number of containers moved per hour. In New York it's twenty-five, while Norfolk, Charleston, New Orleans, and Houston are close to forty. Northern European ports are in the upper thirties. Antwerp's fantastic crane operators are discharging containers before all the ship's lines are tied-up. Livorno is good at thirty, but Egypt is slow at twelve moves per hour. Discharge and loading is computerized, so that trucks are lined up in the order of the containers, an example of the infrastructure need to move containers.

Captain Wanner:

In 1976, I sailed on the *SS Sam Houston*, a LASH (Lighter Aboard Ship) vessel of the Waterman Steamship Company. She was 986 feet long with a beam of ninety feet. Eighty-three LASH barges, each sixty feet long and thirty feet wide with a capacity of 500 tons, were taken aboard through the stern of the ship.

The LASH concept originated with large, amphibious, naval vessels and was applied to commercial vessels in an attempt to offset costs. It became prohibitively expensive because the barges were costly and had to be maintained and reused. To be effective a LASH vessel must go from a complete river system to a discharge port where the barge can move in a river system to its destination. A good example is loading grain into a barge at a grain elevator in the Midwestern U.S., towing the barge to New Orleans, loading it onto a LASH vessel, discharging it in Rotterdam and towing it, via a river system, to its final destination. Unfortunately, the freight rate for grain does not justify the expensive LASH equipment.

At Juncion, the pilot station for Buenos Aires, I observed the operational problems posed by LASH. The cost of towing the barges from the vessel to the port was so high that it exceeded the cost of going alongside a dock to discharge our cargo. But I also saw an example of how LASH is supposed to work. On a return voyage, the *Sam Houston* called at Assab, Ethiopia, a tiny port at the southern end of the Red Sea, for six LASH barges loaded with 3,000 tons of coffee. We anchored outside the breakwater, loaded the waiting six barges, and were underway again in under four hours. It would have taken up to seven days to load alongside a dock in Assab. The *Sam Houston* carried only LASH barges and could work her cargoes at an anchorage without ever having to go alongside a dock. Containers made up the forward third of the cargo capacities of Prudential Lines' and Delta Lines' LASH vessels. A small, on-board crane handled those containers, losing the advantage of being able to work from an anchorage.

The U.S. Lines' containership *SS American Trader* was originally a Pacific Far East Lines LASH ship. Her square blunt stern, built to allow barges to be brought in and lifted, made for large fuel consumption.

In New York all cargo enters the port by truck and has to be hand-stowed into barges for loading onto a LASH vessel, forfeiting any savings in stevedoring costs. The less-costly alternative is loading the cargo into an ocean-going container at the factory. In my opinion, this shows that the containership, with its instant over-the-road capability, is superior to LASH because it is an extension of road or railroad transportation links.

Mr. Bullock:

In 1997, after I'd been going to sea for over ten years, the MM&P opened the books to new members. My first job was a relief trip on the only U.S. asphalt carrier, Sargent Marine's *SS Asphalt Commander*, on her run from Venezuela to Miami, Norfolk and Baltimore.

I really enjoy sailing Second Mate on Central Gulf Lines' car carriers, the motor vessels *Green Point* and *Green Lake*, each built in the mid-1980s, about 500 feet long, about 20,000 gross tons, with a crew of twenty two. In a four and half-month cycle each ship runs empty from New York to Toyahashi, Japan, an industry city near Nagoya. There stevedores drive 5000 New Toyota automobiles aboard, park them four inches apart, and shackle them down. The mates' main job is checking the shackling. On two trips Toyotas are delivered to Portland, Oregon and Los Angles and on the third trip to Jacksonville, Florida, Baltimore and New York. I made a trip in 1998 and one in 1999. MM&P rules require that mates get off after 120 days and wait a minimum of sixty days before bidding on another job. Every day I'm at the 1:00 P.M. call at MM&P's New York Hall in hopes of getting back on the *Green Point* or *Green Lake*.

WARTIME

Captain Carter:

I returned to sea on Christmas Day, 1942, as Chief Mate of the Liberty Ship *William Eaton*, named after the U.S. Consul to Tunis who stormed a fort in Libya with U.S. Marines in 1804. I made three trips in North Atlantic convoys in 1943, as Master on the second and third trips. In one convoy of forty-seven ships, twenty-eight reached Halifax, Nova Scotia. The rest were blown off course or sunk.

The English Channel had been closed for two years. With two other Liberties the *Eaton* ran it with cargo for Plymouth, England. The Liberties and our escorts were all instructed to scatter if we encountered any German E-Boats. Fortunately, none appeared.

On a return trip we carried 300 German prisoners of war (POWs), men of General Rommel's Africa Corps, because it was easier to feed them in the U.S. Six or eight U.S. Army men guarded them. These U.S. soldiers had accumulated enough combat points to go home, so the Germans respected them. The *Eaton's* twenty five-man U.S. Navy Armed Guard also watched the POWs.

The prisoners slept on straw mattresses in the cargo holds and came up on deck for fresh air one at a time. All of them expected to die, believing that the *Eaton* would be torpedoed by German U-Boats.

German Army cooks prepared their meals on two gas stoves on deck. A delegation asked me to permit prisoners who had been cooks in civilian life to do the cooking because they were far better. I agreed.

Using chocolate bars the crew paid a German who had been a barber, to cut their hair. It seemed strange to have a prisoner with a straight razor trimming my hair.

On arrival at the Staten Island, New York Army Base my crew was not going to be permitted ashore until all the prisoners were examined. I informed the U.S. Army people that it was illegal to hold U.S. sailors after completion of a voyage. They found me personally "free of infestation" and did not examine the crew nor prisoners. They just did not want to clear the ship because we had arrived late in their workday.

On one voyage, a Chinese cook complained of stomach pains and asked to get off to see a Chinese doctor in New York. I sent a message to an escort ship to recommend treatment, adding my suspicion that he was what we called a dope fiend. The escort's reply was, "Give him dope."

Luckily, the *Eaton* was never damaged. During the war, my address was 3113 Weaver Avenue, Baltimore. All my convoy numbers were variations of this address, for example, 113. I've played these numbers in the Maryland Lottery, but must have used up all my luck.

Captain Atkinson:

In 1940, I was Second Mate on the *SS Florence Luckenbach* discharging general cargo in Basra, Iraq. A pro-Nazi element was fighting British Indian troops. The rebels set a river ferry afire. It floated past us so close that I felt the heat, but did no damage to us.

After I got my Chief Mate's license in February 1942, the MM&P dispatcher talked me into taking a short coastwise trip as Third Mate on the 7335-ton tanker *SS William C. McTarnahan*. On May 16, 1942, I was still on her, as Second Mate, en route in water ballast from New York to Port Isabel, Texas.

I had just come off the twelve to four A.M. watch and was undressing for bed. At 4:12 A.M., west of the the Southwest Pass of the Mississippi River, an area of the Gulf of Mexico thought "safe," the German submarine U-506 hit the *McTarnahan* with a torpedo, followed seconds later by another one. All lights and power went out, and the ship took a heavy list to starboard.

Chief Mate George O.C. Midgett had seen two torpedo tracks 200 yards off the starboard bow and shouted to the Quartermaster, "Hard right!" The first torpedo struck the Number 2 cargo tank, forward on the starboard side, immediately flooding that tank. The second torpedo penetrated the after peak tank, the steering engine room, and the main engine room, killing all there in a blaze.

I ran to my lifeboat station aft. We carried two lifeboats swung out aft and two life rafts amidships. The force of the second explosion carried away the after falls of both lifeboats, leaving them hanging vertically by their forward falls. Nearly all the equipment in the boats had come adrift and was lost. The explosion ignited the ship's fuel tanks aft, and the after part of the ship was an inferno.

I had the lifeboat's forward falls slacked off, two men slide down the falls into the boat, and sent men forward to haul the boat amidships. Our list brought the ship's main deck on the starboard side to within only seven or eight feet of the water. The injured easily embarked into the lifeboat. When the boat was filled, Captain John G. Leech ordered me to cast off. Before we could get clear, the submarine commenced shelling, but we escaped being hit.

No distress signal could be sent since the main and auxiliary antennas were destroyed, and power failed. Our U.S. Navy Armed Guard could not return fire because the four-inch gun aft was put out of action by the explosion, and flames drove the gun crew away.

After daybreak, fishing boats picked up the survivors and took them ashore to a hospital at Houma, Louisiana.

Several severely burned men in my boat told me a flash of flame swept through the ship's passageway and quarters, searing everybody in its path. Those trapped in their quarters were cremated. The skin on the arms and hands of Bosun Thomas W. Murray peeled off like a long pair of gloves and was hanging from his fingertips. He and the AB on my watch, John F. Jenkins, lived about two weeks. Second Assistant Engineer Virgil J. Meroney was burned in his room. He and Second Cook Ora Ellis died soon after landing ashore. Half the merchant crew, nineteen men, died.

The *McTarnahan* did not sink, was repaired, and put back in service.

There has been much adverse publicity by individuals and organizations about merchant mariners being grossly overpaid during the war. My pay as Second Mate, the Navigating Officer, was $205 per month. When the *McTarnahan* was torpedoed, I was earning a war zone bonus of about $70 a month, less than the cost of the watch and other items I lost.

In July 1942, I shipped as Second Mate on my first Liberty Ship, the *Benjamin Chew*, under construction in Baltimore. When my friend, Third Mate Joe Beck, and I arrived at the shipyard, the *Benjamin Chew* was only a midship section on the ways. Within a month, she had her sea trials, and we were en route to New York for loading.

We went through the Panama Canal and around Cape Horn, the only time I've gone around the Horn, then proceded due east to the longitude of Capetown, South Africa and then north for discharge at Capetown, East London, and Durban, South Africa.

Life aboard was relaxed and monotonous. Boat and gun drills were little more than slow, grumbling walks to stations. The U.S. Navy Armed Guard Lieutenant complained to me about the crew's poor performance. I suggested that he put more realism into the drills by firing one of his guns before sounding the alarm. Captain Andrew Anderson, a fine old gentleman from the Shetland Islands, gave his approval. We stationed some reliable men at the lifeboats to control possible panic and fired the three-inch gun. Within seconds, all hands reported to their stations, clothed and unclothed, some wet and soapy from showers and others wrapped in bedclothes. There was no panic. I think that they enjoyed it, especially after finding out it was just a drill. Afterward, morale and participation in drills vastly improved.

On the return voyage, in the middle of the Atlantic, we saw two men-of-war and first thought that they were German raiders. Luckily, one was American and the other Brazilian.

We loaded a cargo of bauxite at Paranam, Dutch Guyana, topped off in Port of Spain, Trinidad and sailed in convoy to New York. A Staten Island ferry ran into the *Benjamin Chew* during the twelve to four A.M. watch, while we were at anchor in fog in New York Harbor. Our only damage was a bent rail.

In March 1943, I joined the U.S. Army Transport *Alamo* as First Officer. She was a small, World War I Great Lakes vessel. Additional armor made her top-heavy, so stone ballast was carried in the lower holds. We shuttled between Australia and New Guinea with meats, butter, and eggs in reefer spaces in the tween decks and vehicles, gasoline in drums, and foodstuffs, like potatoes, on deck. At the end of articles, I paid-off in Brisbane in February 1944, and returned to San Francisco as a passenger on another ship.

In June 1944, I joined the U.S. Maritime Service with the rank of Lieutenant Commander, went to upgrading school in Baltimore, and obtained my Master's license.

The T-2 was a new tanker then. I wanted to be Master of one, so I went as Chief Mate on the T-2 *SS Fisher's Hill*. After two trips to the United Kingdom with aviation gas, I didn't get promoted, so paid-off.

Captain Matt Coward was Port Captain for Black Diamond Lines in New York. I had sailed with him as a cadet in 1934, when he was Second Mate on the *SS Black Falcon*. In October 1944 Coward sent me to Baltimore to take command of the Liberty Ship *William Grayson*. His parting words were, "From now on, Bill, you'll be swinging on your own hook!" Captain Coward was the first Master of the *SS John W. Brown*, a Liberty Ship I'm helping to restore in Baltimore.

The *William Grayson* was the first Chief's job for the Chief Engineer. He was reluctant to give me speed, so maintaining our station in the Atlantic convoy was difficult. We anchored with about fifty Liberties in the Solent, behind the Isle of Wight in England, then were suddenly ordered to LeHavre to discharge our cargo for the Battle of the Bulge.

Leaving LeHavre, a ship ahead either hit a mine or was torpedoed. I told the Chief Engineer what happened and asked for more revolutions on the engine. I never had a problem with that Chief and speed again.

Ships in the return convoy loaded slag into their holds and tween decks at Barry, Wales as ballast. One of the Black Diamond skippers had worked out the trim calculations for this ballast, and we all followed them.

On my second trip as Master, in an eastbound convoy in fair visibility at 1:03 A.M. on March 18, 1945, the *Grayson* collided bow to bow with the British Steamship *Empire Lord.* The ships then swung parallel to each other. Rolling in the seaway and trying to get clear, the *Empire Lord* struck our starboard quarter. The *Grayson's* starboard bow was stove in twenty-seven feet back from the stem and from the lower end of the hawse pipe upward. Her main deck was pushed in about two feet. Eight frames and eight beams in the starboard bow buckled and bent. About twelve feet of the starboard side aft were dented in about six inches. There were no injuries and no damage below the water line. The *Grayson* was later turned over to Greek interests to replace ships they had lost.

I transferred to the new Liberty Ship *William R. Lewis,* sailed independently to Casablanca and Naples, and was en route to the Pacific when Japan surrendered.

In the Philippines we loaded Army cargo and thirty-five Army and Navy passengers for New Orleans. During the passage from Enewetok to the Panama Canal, we bucked trade winds practically the whole distance, 7063 miles in thirty-one days at an average speed of only 9.42 knots.

The *Lewis* returned to commercial service, but I had difficulty getting a full crew. Only my friend, Chief Mate

Joe Beck, and an engineer remained from the previous voyage. Once the war ended, there was a general shortage of crews.

In 1953, during the Korean War, as Master of the Liberty Ship *John Paul Jones*, I carried military vehicles from Philadelphia to Inchon, Korea. On later trips we took cargoes of coal from Sasebo, Japan to Kunsan, Korea and wheat from the U.S. to Inchon. On her return to the U.S., the ship was laid-up.

Captain Fowler:

When Pearl Harbor was bombed on December 7, 1941, I was employed as a First Class Rigger at Sparrows Point Shipyard in Baltimore. I knew that I had to go back to sea or wait for the Navy to call me. On December 8th, I quit my job at the shipyard. On December 9th, I was reinstated in the MM&P. That evening an old friend called me to go as Second Mate on a passenger vessel with him as Third Mate. The inducement was that we could have our pick of the quarters. The next morning, the Port Captain hired us with all the benefits and wages the MM&P called for. It sounded too good to be true, and it certainly was. When I went to the pier in Locust Point, my heart sank. After working at the shipyard on brand new ships with all the latest gear, I was going to sea in the *SS Ponce* under the Panamanian flag. She was built in 1898, one of the old Puerto Rico Lines' passenger ships in New York to Puerto Rico service.

The Captain was a U.S. citizen of Norwegian descent. The Chief Engineer was a U.S. citizen of Chilean descent. Two engineers were Dutch. One engineer, the Oilers and Firemen were Spanish. The members of the Steward's Department were British. The Chief Mate, Radio Operator and deck crew were Canadians, except for one American AB and one American Ordinary. I decided to make the best of it, but get off after a round trip with coal for Clarenville, New Foundland.

We departed Baltimore on December 11 th, and had a fair voyage with our running lights on all the way. How were we to know that a German Submarine Wolf Pack was on its way? The coal was discharged over Christmas in waist-high snow.

We stopped in St. Johns, New Foundland for a while, then loaded Army cargo, beer, cigarettes, and trucks, at Halifax, Nova Scotia for Africa. We sailed directly south to Trinidad with no trouble from the Wolf Packs operating off the Grand Banks, then due east to Freetown, Sierra Leone. During two weeks waiting in port, the Chief Mate and Chief Engineer did a lot of name-calling. The Chief Mate left the ship, and I became Chief Mate.

We received orders to proceed to Matadi, a small port about eighty miles up the Congo River in the Belgian Congo. Halfway down the coast, at about 2 P.M., the Second Mate sounded the general alarm after a ship exploded and went down a mile off our starboard beam. A German submarine surfaced. We swung out the lifeboats, but were not fired on, possibly because of our Panamanian flag. We later learned that five ships were sunk within fifty miles of us that day.

We returned to Matadi and lay at anchor for almost two weeks before a boat took the Captain to a convoy meeting. About 6 P.M., he returned with a stack of books and put them on my desk. He said that all he knew was that we were to leave at six the following morning. He was a little deaf and couldn't hear all that was said at the conference. The Second Mate, Radio Operator, and myself spent the next four hours studying the convoy orders and signal flags.

As soon as the anchor was heaved up the following morning, the Captain called me to the bridge. He said, "Well, you got her." and went to his quarters.

I raised our number, forty-one, with signal flags and proceeded at about eight knots. When we got a little ahead or back of our position with relation to the other ships in the convoy, I called the Engine Room to either

slow down or speed up the revolutions. Ev
fine when the Second Mate relieved me at noon.

I was napping in my quarters about 2 P.M.,
heard the engine room telegraph. The engine
stopped, the Chief Engineer was shouting to the Secon
Mate from the Boat Deck, and the convoy was a mile
astern of us. It developed that during my morning watch,
the Chief Engineer told the Third Assistant Engineer to
ignore my orders, and he telephoned speed instructions to
him from the Promenade Deck. The Chief Engineer took a
nap after lunch, and the relieving engineer continued to
ignore bridge orders, so the Second Mate finally ordered
the ship stopped. The convoy caught up with us, and we
resumed our position.

That night the convoy made a sharp zig-zag turn and
increased speed to nine knots, leaving us well behind. I
headed directly for the rendezvous position and caught up
to the convoy by daylight.

We loaded copper ingots and coffee at Takoradi, Ivory
Coast for Halifax and proceeded independently to Trinidad,
where we joined a convoy to Key West. By this time, we
were good at maintaining our position, and the crew could
read convoy flag hoists. While anchored at Key West, I
saw my first Liberty Ship, loaded deep, guns and Naval
Gun Crew aboard, painted gray, and clean. I wanted to
get on one as soon as I could leave the *Ponce*.

The convoy arrived Hampton Roads, where a Navy
Commander came aboard looking for me. When he asked
whether I intended to stay in the Merchant Marine, I
thought that I would be in the Navy that day. I explained
that I intended to get off at Halifax and take an American
ship out of Baltimore. He replied, "OK, but get yourself a
decent ship."

We next anchored in the Delaware Bay. On departure,
mine was designated the Vice Commodore ship in the
convoy to New York, up the East River, Long Island
Sound, Cape Cod Canal, and then by ourselves to Halifax.

… per 1942, after a ten-month voyage, … to Baltimore.

…tes gathered at a nautical instrument … Street in Baltimore. There I met the …erican Foreign Steamship Corporation. … Chief Mate on the Liberty Ship *Ralph* …ed at Locust Point. After three days, … to the Liberty Ship *David Stone*, still on the ways. … and I stayed at the Cape Fear Hotel in Wilmington, North Carolina waiting for my ship to be built. The other officers took rooms at the same hotel, and we had many a party after a day on the ship. My wife and the Third Mate's wife became very close. After the war, when I was a Master, he was my Chief Mate. We'd sometimes stay with them in New York.

The Master of the *David Stone* was Peter J. Frantzen, a look-alike for the silent film star Wallace Beery. I had sailed as Second Mate in the Calmar Line with his father. Pete and I remained good friends until his death in the 1970s.

In December 1942, we sailed for Charleston, South Carolina, loaded Army cargo, and left shortly after Christmas to join a convoy at Key West. Two Canadian corvettes escorted the us and the Liberty Ship *Benjamin K. Smith*, via Trinidad, to Takoradi. We anchored off the coast of Liberia for a few hours to discharge mail and then continued alone to Takoradi. We learned the next day that the *Smith* was sunk on its way to Takoradi, but the crew got ashore.

We discharged our deck cargo of boats and took on boxed airplanes from another ship in the harbor. My crew had to do all the securing of the deck cargo. My experience as a rigger came in handy.

After discharging the rest of our cargo in Karachi, we proceeded to Calcutta for a full load of coal. Men and women with baskets of coal on their heads walked up a plank at each hatch, dumped the coal into the hatch, and returned to the dock by another plank. At the end of the day, they took baths just astern of the ship. I had to stop the Gun Crew from throwing them bars of soap because we couldn't get supplies. Around-the-clock loading of the coal took two weeks.

Japanese cruisers were rumored to be in the Bay of Bengal, but we didn't see them. Sailing via the Red Sea and Suez Canal, we spent a few days in Alexandria, Egypt then went on to Malta in a heavily escorted convoy. We discharged half the coal there, working only during the day due to the nighttime blackout.

We discharged the other half of the coal at Alexandria and took on a full cargo for the British Eighth Army. The British ship *Fishpool* was loading at the other side of the pier. In convoy with escorts we departed, the *David Stone* for Augusta, Sicily and the *Fishpool* for Syracuse, Sicily.

On arrival in Augusta, we heard gunfire. In the outer harbor we finally found a place among many naval vessels to drop the hook. We soon got a message from a British cruiser, "You'll have to move. You're in line with my guns." We quickly found another anchorage. On my watch, shortly after 4 A.M., every vessel in the harbor, except us, fired for about a half-hour, covering the sky with red tracers. This was our baptism of fire.

The next morning, a naval officer guided the *David Stone* to a dock in Augusta's inner harbor. A boatload of British soldiers came aboard to discharge our cargo. We docked in the daytime and returned to the anchorage at night. That evening, I was on the bow heaving up the anchor. A German plane came out of the western sky with the sun behind him, and dropped a bomb. Every day for seventeen days, a German plane came out of the east in the morning and the west at night and dropped a bomb. One bomb fell close enough to splash water on our side. Our Naval Gun Crew waited for the German plane's arrival, but shot only at a British plane not supposed to fly over the area. A Navy anti-aircraft barge stayed near us during discharge operations.

A British Army Captain with about fifteen men sailed from Alexandria with us. On the second night in Augusta, after the German plane had flown down to Syracuse, we saw the flare of a big explosion in that direction. The next day, the British Captain went ashore for orders and came back very upset. The *SS Fishpool* had been blown up in Syracuse with the rest of his men on her.

At the end of one day's discharging, a British soldier boarded the shore boat without his rifle. His Sergeant made him climb back up the pilot ladder and down into Number 3 Hold for his rifle, while the boat waited. The boat was halfway to the dock when a German plane dropped its bomb. It landed on the dock where the soldiers' boat tied up every night. Waiting for the forgetful soldier saved them all.

We departed Augusta in a convoy headed west. About 9 P.M. one night, I was talking with some people on the Boat Deck. The Third Mate shouted from the wing of the bridge that a plane was coming in from ahead, and then a lot of planes. By the time I ran up to the bridge, the Captain was in the wheelhouse. Our forward escorts were all firing at very low-flying Henkel 111 torpedo planes. Then all the ships in the convoy began firing. The coast of Spain was visible. They had evidently come from there. We were the second ship in our line. From the starboard wing of the bridge the Third Mate and I watched one of the planes drop a torpedo. It ran ten feet off our starboard side and struck the bow of the ship astern of us.

After the planes went down our lines, they reformed and came back at us from the port side. One had been hit. It just cleared our main mast, and I could see the faces of the two flyers. As their plane hit the water between the *David Stone* and the next ship, its tail went up in the air. I was busy, looked elsewhere, and then no longer saw it.

On anchoring in Gibraltar harbor the next day, we learned that ten planes had been downed and three ships hit by torpedoes. I never learned what happened to those ships. The planes were probably after the loaded convoy that we passed earlier and made a terrible mistake in attacking us.

In the three days we were at Gib, we had to pass a line under the ship from the port bow to the starboard quarter. Every watch worked the line port side back and starboard side forward. If the line got stuck, we were to call for divers, who would check for mines. After the war, I read that a ship aground in Spanish waters at the head of the bay was a base for German divers to attach mines to the hulls of anchored ships.

We arrived in New York in September 1943. Before paying-off, I asked Morris Ginsberg, one of the owners of American Foreign Steamship Corporation, for a Master's job. After waiting at home for six weeks, I stopped in at the Calmar Line offices in New York and was immediately sent to Boston to relieve the Captain of the *SS Kenmar*. Two weeks later, Calmar offered me the job of Captain of the *SS Flomar*, but I wouldn't take it. The bulkheads between Numbers 2 and 3 and 4 and 5 holds had been removed to carry long steel bridge parts to California, so the old *Flomar* would go right down if hit by a torpedo.

In December 1943, American Foreign assigned me as Master of the Liberty Ship *Morris Sheppard* being outfitted in Houston. My wife and I took a room at the Sam Houston Hotel.

My sister told me that my father would be buried at 2 P.M. on February 3, 1943. At 1 P.M. that day, I was signing acceptance papers at the shipyard, so I could not get home. We sailed for New Orleans at 5 P.M. This was the first time I had a gyrocompass. On my first night in a Master's job, we got through thick fog off the coast by proceeding at dead slow speed and using Radio Direction Finder bearings to anchor just off the bell buoy. Soon it cleared up, and a Mississippi River Pilot came aboard to take us up the river.

Third Mate Joe Rulewich had been a Kings Point Cadet with me on the *SS David Stone* and turned into a fine watch officer on the *Morris Sheppard*.

We sailed from New Orleans in convoy with general cargo for San Juan, Puerto Rico, discharged there, took on a half-load of sugar at Encinada, and finished loading sugar at Mayaguez on the west coast of Puerto Rico.

We proceeded to New York in convoy, discharged, and took on a full cargo of coal at Newport News.

In convoy we sailed for Santos, Brazil. Discharging the coal and loading a full cargo of coffee took twenty-one days. What a fine place for liberty! I took a room at the Atlantica Hotel and went to the ship each day for four or five hours. In the evenings, two mates, the Gunnery Officer, Purser, Radio Operator, and myself went to a fine beach restaurant featuring orchestras and beautiful dancing girls. We were in Santos on D-Day.

We proceeded to Rio de Janiero. My ship was designated the Navy Commodore's up the coast to Trinidad. He wanted as many fixes for positions as possible during the voyage. I took the sights, and Joe, my Third Mate, took the times of them on my mark. I worked out each sight and gave the result to Joe. He plotted each to establish our position for the Commodore. Daily at noon, the Commodore had our fix before any other ships ran up their positions with signal flags. We got an "A" for navigation in that convoy.

At Trinidad we joined another convoy and sailed for New York.

We made two routine voyages, one from Wilmington, North Carolina and the other from Newport News, to Marseilles with full military cargoes. Returning on the second voyage, half the convoy went to the East Coast and half to the Gulf. My orders were to Caimanera. After a lot of checking through books and charts, I found this small port up in Guantanamo Bay, Cuba. We loaded a full cargo of sugar for Gulfport, Mississippi, where I was relieved on March 31, 1945.

When I got home for vacation, my wife told me that a notice to appear for my medical exam for induction into the Army had arrived, followed by a telephone call wanting to know why I had not appeared. She replied that I was the Captain of a Liberty Ship, probably somewhere in the Atlantic Ocean. My Draft Board told her to forget it.

As Master of the *SS Nathan Clifford* I took on almost a full cargo at Providence, Rhode Island, went through the Panama Canal, and topped off with cargo at Balboa. We sailed alone for the Philippines. One evening, we received a message to change course quite a bit because a Japanese submarine was thought to be directly ahead of our course. About 10 P.M., on a starless cloudy night, a red blinker light off our starboard beam asked our identification signal. I figured that it was a U.S. destroyer and felt better.

After discharging our cargo just inside Leyte Gulf on the south coast of Samar Island, I was ordered to Enewetak for bunkers. I proceeded through many Navy ships to a small docked tanker. A large troop ship was fueling on the tanker's starboard side. I had never docked a ship by myself. The wind was a steady force five or six. My ship was light, so I couldn't let the wind get too far on either side of my bow. I approached the tanker at half-ahead speed, then half astern, using the wheel to steer when the course fell off slightly. I came alongside that tanker so easy that I never touched it until I was in position. The Chief Mate quickly got out breast lines to hold us to the tanker. The Second Mate got lines out at the forward end of Number 4 hatch, which was as far as the tanker extended. A Navy man on the tanker asked me to move forward fifteen feet, which I did with no problem. After we were tied up, I noticed that the troop ship's bridge was completely covered with officers and the lower decks with soldiers, all watching me. I was on the bridge wing wearing an old cap, the Third Mate was in the Pilot House doorway, and an AB was on the wheel. I waved, no shouting, to the Chief and Second Mates to secure the lines, ordered the engine room to stop the engines, and begin taking on oil.

I was following a great circle course to San Francisco, just north of the Hawaiian Islands, when the bomb was dropped on Japan. The celebration was still going on when we arrived in San Francisco. Most of my crew paid-off there.

Vietnam was my next war. In 1966, I quit Calmar Line, went to the MM&P Hall in Baltimore, and the next day, got a job relieving the Master of the *SS Lakewood Victory* at Tampa. She was owned by the U.S. Government and operated by American Foreign Steamship Corporation. We loaded general cargo at Brownsville, Texas, New Orleans, and Mobile, including a deck cargo of telephone poles, for Vietnam. We laid at anchor in Manila for about three weeks awaiting orders, were sent to Cam Ranh Bay, waited a week at anchor, and went to Da Nang, where the poles were discharged. The remainder of the cargo was discharged back at Cam Ranh Bay.

On the return voyage, off the coast of Lower California, we lost a foot off the propeller blade and continued at slightly reduced speed to ease the vibrations. A few days later, another foot of the same propeller fell off. We were permitted to transit the Panama Canal. At a dock in Colon shore personnel burned off part of the opposite blade. We proceeded at reduced speed to New Orleans, where a new propeller was to be installed. The permanent Master returned, and I went home.

Two weeks later, American Foreign offered me a job on the *SS Wellesly Victory* in Baltimore. I relieved the Master the same day and sailed late that night for Boston. After loading a full cargo, we sailed for Vietnam.

After returning from Vietnam, I was on the *SS Gretna Victory* for a short time.

On July 19, 1968, I went to the *SS Oshkosh Victory* and eventually became permanent Master. We carried full cargoes of ammunition from Wilmington, North Carolina, a munitions port just west of Sandy Hook, New Jersey, Port Bangor in Puget Sound, and Port Chicago near San

Francisco, to Vietnam. Once fifty tons of explosives were aboard, a bonus of ten percent was paid to the crew.

Occasional shelling took place, and a bonus was paid for that day. At midnight, discharging ammunition from five hatches in Qui Nhon, Vietnam, a U.S. Marine awakened me to order everyone to leave the ship. Mortars on a hill began firing at the ship. The shells were falling short, but the stevedores ran off. An hour later, after the shelling stopped, the stevedores returned to work.

Captain White:

We were living in Redondo Beach, California near the oil port of San Pedro, during World War II, so I shipped out on tankers. I was on a "milk run" to Pearl Harbor and the South Pacific, islands like Kwajalein, Majura, Pago Pago, and Tutuila, wherever the fleet needed Bunker C.

I didn't particularly like sailing on tankers because they tied up at awful tank farms and refineries, out of the real world. But they were comfortable at sea, more spacious quarters and better food because of the fast turnaround.

I never worked on a passenger ship, but met one interesting passenger during World War II. As Second Mate on the tanker *SS Pequod Hill*, I finished discharging at Bora Bora, French Oceania. An excited U.S. Army Major, who I later learned had been an attorney in Rhode Island, came aboard from a launch. He brought with him a Mr. Hall, suntanned, wearing a felt hat, and carrying a carpenter's chest and beat-up bicycle. I introduced Mr. Hall to our very nice Captain, Oscar Lund.

Mr. Hall was the author James Norman Hall, collaborator with Charles Nordhoff on the trilogy *Mutiny on the Bounty, Men Against the Sea*, and *Pitcairn Island*. His wife and daughter had already left on a tanker, and Hall was going back to San Pedro with us. I suspected that Hall did intelligence work for the U.S. in the South Pacific.

During the voyage, Hall told us that he had been out of the U.S. for twenty-four years. After working at

97

barnstorming aviation back home in Iowa, he enlisted in the Canadian Forces in World War I. Flying in the Lafayette Espadrille he was wounded in France. Charles Nordhoff was in the next hospital bed, and they decided to look for adventure together. After reading about the South Seas, they bought round-trip tickets on a steamer from San Francisco to Papeete, Tahiti.

In Tahiti they met a retired British Navy Captain who suggested that they write about a mutiny on a British ship called the *Bounty*. He got transcripts of the trial in England for them. Hall and Nordhoff chartered a sailing vessel to Pitcairn Island to interview descendants of the *Bounty's* survivors. They developed too much information for one book, so wrote two books, and then the famous trilogy. The movie version of *Mutiny on the Bounty* brought Hall and Nordhoff financial success. Hall was a friendly man and gave us the manuscript of his book *Lost Horizon* to read. After the voyage, he sent Captain Lund and me copies of the books in the trilogy. The Hall family remains prominent in Tahiti.

By age twenty-six, I had accumulated experience as Third, Second, and Chief Mate and was given command of the Liberty Ship *Frank Adair Monroe* in the South Pacific. You never forget the first ship you command. I'm still in contact with the Chief Mate, who was a classmate at Alameda, and the Chief Steward.

I did not have any harrowing experiences during the war. A friend of mine was Captain of a Moran deep-sea tug at a dock in London during a bombing. The impact slammed him against the bridge and broke both his jaws. He still had mouth and teeth trouble years later.

We were allowed two days ashore for every seven on a ship. The Purser mailed a card to each crewman's Draft Board when he paid-off. If he overstayed his shore leave, a sailor could be drafted into the Army.

I blame World War II's newcomers to the Merchant Marine for the bad publicity about us being paid so much.

They had never had anything before the war, so, after a ship paid-off, bragged about their big money.

Captain McCarthy:

I was the Deck Cadet on Moore McCormack's *SS Mormacmoon*, a C-3 cargo ship built in 1940. With Captain Jesse R. Hodges and Chief Mate John T. Larsen, later Superintendent of Marine Operations for Mormac, we sailed on August 4, 1942 with a full load of military cargo for Capetown, South Africa. To prevent German submarine attacks we sailed as fast as possible, zig-zagging during the day. Along with the watch officer, the Captain and Chief Mate took eight-hour turns on the bridge.

A storm with rollers from the Cape of Good Hope split the deck aft of Number 3 hatch. The three-inch crack was lashed with chains and wire, patched with cement, and caulked. We met cape rollers again at anchor in Durban for fuel.

We proceeded safely to Aden for fuel, although there were submarines in the Mozambique Channel. The deck cargo of tanks and aircraft were unloaded at Port Sudan. Unloading the ammunition into barges at Suez and Port Tewfik, Egypt took thirty days.

Instead of returning to New York, the ship was turned over to the British Transport Service. In mid-October, 1942, we began loading at Port Sudan for a secret destination - ammunition in Number One hold, five-gallon cans of high-octane gasoline in Numbers Two and Three, food in Number Four, and coal in Number Five hold. The American ship *Robin Locksley*, the Dutch ship *Bataan*, and the British ship *Devingshire* were also loading.

All four ships sailed for Mohammed Gul, Saudi Arabia, and on to Suez. En route we drilled in large lifeboats with push-pull propulsion handles. With the wind off the desert, it was difficult to get back to the ship. I prefer oars.

Mormac's agent in Suez, a Maltese, refused to tell us our destination, but said that he did not think we would return. The column of four ships cleared the Suez Canal at night on November 16, 1942, and was joined by a British escort of two battleships, an aircraft carrier, ten heavy cruisers, anti-aircraft cruisers, numerous destroyers, and land-based and carrier-based planes. The mine-laying cruiser *Manxman* could drop mines at thirty knots. We learned that our destination was Malta, where they were starving. If one of the four ships got through, they could hold the island. Battle conditions were in effect twenty-four hours a day with attacks by German dive-bombers, torpedo bombers, and Italian E-boats.

I quote from Captains Hodges' and Larsen's history of this voyage, *The Sun Never Sets on the Mormacmoon*:

"On the second day, November 18, the convoy was spotted by the enemy. At 11:15 attacked by five Junker 88s flying directly overhead. Five bombs dropped in near vicinity of vessel, shaking vessel heavy.

....darkness came, cruisers took up formation about two miles astern of the merchant ships...other vessels formed close by, in readiness for a torpedo attack ....

Just as the last light was leaving the west....torpedo attacking planes...discharged all their torpedoes in the cruiser formation....one of the cruisers received a torpedo...and lost 129 men....next day came in with strong gales, rain and heavy overcast which discouraged further enemy attacks.

Convoy zigzagged day and night at 15 knots in a very close formation. Emergency turns of 90 degrees...on light and whistle signals....danger of sinking by collision was as great as any....Captain Hodges or myself...always on the flying bridge along with the watch officers with our binoculars trained on the wake of the vessel ahead continuously as there were no lights on any vessel....

On November 20, the convoy entered the harbor of Valetta, Malta single file to find a complete blackout....shore was lined with cheering people...Lord

Gott, Governor of Malta, and his staff came
followed by hundreds of soldiers who proceeded to u
the vital supplies."

Submarine nets were opened for the convoy to enter
the harbor, closed after us, and depth charges were
dropped in case any submarines followed. Wrecked ships
were everywhere. The shipyard had been destroyed.

During frequent air raids we abandoned ship for air raid
shelters ashore.

"Soldiers keeled over from the fumes while unloading
the high-octane gas...air raid signals went off every three
hours or so...a soldier would hurry down a ladder into the
hold, place two cans on a pallet and run up...until the pallet
was ready to be taken out...loose gasoline was two feet in
the hold...no one slept until it had been pumped into the
drums and the bilges flooded with water to let out the gas
fumes."

The Sun Never Sets on the Mormac Moon

We sailed for Suez on December 7, 1942. What a
difference in my life in one year!

"Bound for Suez with a smaller escort fleet, the convoy
was attacked the first day out by torpedo-carrying planes.
One officer and two ratings were killed...on the naval
escort....Next day, just as the flags were being lowered for
funeral exercises for these men, five Junkers 88s attacked
again, dropping three bombs....five more attacked...a
single escorting Spitfire engaged a whole squadron of
Junkers, bringing down two....the trip back from Malta was
even rougher than the trip out.

...at 5:40 P.M...attacked by a squadron of the same
planes. Bombs dropped in the near vicinity of the
vessel....a lone Junker came in close overhead...dropped
his bombs which fell about 150 feet astern...shaking the
vessel extremely heavy.

A destroyer escort made contact with an enemy
submarine and dropped depth charges less than a half

hip....December 11...reached Port Said...all
re and without damage to the vessel or her
ry officer and man did his duty in a manner
with the traditions of the sea.
aid the Mormacmoon sailed for Mombasa,

The Sun Never Sets on the Mormacmoon

My log for December 25, 1942 reads, "At sea. Merry Christmas! Like hell!"

I went ashore with a Gunner's Mate in Mombasa. The buses wouldn't stop, and we couldn't find a ricksha. We ran back to the ship for a midnight sailing. Only her bowline was still ashore, and they brought us aboard in the eye of it.

On December 29th, off Dar es Salaam, Tanzania we sighted two submarines, but had no trouble.

My log for December 30th reads, "At sea. Happy Birthday - twenty years old."

On New Year's Day, 1943 we arrived Beira, Portuguese East Africa to load chrome ore. In this neutral country the food was good. We went on safaris. After twenty-one days of loading, we waited for the right combination of a full moon and a high tide to cross the bar to the Mozambique Channel. The Mormacmoon was fast enough to avoid the submarines in the channel and reached Capetown in five days. I bought cake and candy for the trip to New York.

Our convoy of two other cargo ships, a British ex-passenger ship, a cruiser, and destroyers broke up. Captain Hodges told us that we were not going directly to New York, but west through the Straits of Magellan because German raiders had sunk so many ships in the south Atlantic. A pilot took us from Punta Arenas, Chile to Valpariso. The scenery was fantastic. With a transit of the Panama Canal, the voyage of seven months ended in New York on March 6, 1943. I got thirteen days' leave.

I moved up from Deck Cadet to Junior Mate to the Second Officer on the *SS Monterey*, a Matson Line passenger ship being operated as a troop transport for the U.S. Army Transport Service. I made four ten-day trips from Staten Island, New York to Casablanca, Morocco with 8,000 to 10,000 troops each trip. They could have a bunk for only eight hours and ate twice a day at stand-up tables. Coincidentally, in one convoy were Matson's *Monterey*, *Matsonia*, and *Lurline*, Moore McCormack's *Argentina*, *Brazil*, and *Uruguay*, and Grace Line's *Santa Paula* and *Santa Rosa*, all peacetime passenger ships.

The *Monterey* went through the Panama Canal to pick up troops in San Francisco. I got off and got my Third Mate's license at the U.S. Maritime Service School at San Mateo, California.

I joined the MM&P Local 90 in San Francisco and went as Junior Third Mate on the *Mormacwren*, a C1 cargo ship carrying 6,000 to 8,000 troops. In twenty-two days we sailed unescorted and without lights to a staging area at Espiritu Santo in the New Hebrides. We later carried troops to Guadalcanal after the invasion. The stink of death was everywhere.

The U.S. Navy wouldn't allow merchant mariners ashore. Our Navy Gunnery Officer went ashore and brought back some nurses for Thanksgiving dinner. They enjoyed using the ship's showers and wanted toilet paper more than anything. The Captain gave them a case of it.

At Fiji we were advised by blinker light that there was a bottle of liquor for each officer at the British Forces Store. The Captain took my bottle because I was not yet twenty-one years old. I told him that I was old enough to have a license and old enough to have my bottle. He gave it to me, but told me to drink it ashore.

British native troops embarked at Fiji. We loaded their equipment at Espititu Santo and discharged all at Bougainville on D-Day plus three.

Once we left the South Pacific there was no fear of Japanese submarines, but the long trip without running lights or radar was a strain. I had two near-collisions on my watch. The *Mormacwren* arrived San Francisco on December 26, 1943. I turned twenty one on December 30th, and celebrated on New Year's Eve with some classmates at the Palace Hotel.

I preferred East Coast shipping because of the U.S. Navy's attitude toward merchant mariners in the Pacific. In other parts of the world the British Navy controlled the ports and treated merchant mariners as equals. I flew from San Francisco in January 1944, in a cramped DC3 as far as Chicago and took a train the rest of the way to Massachusetts.

On February 9, 1944, as Third Mate I reported aboard the *SS James Fergus*, a Liberty Ship operated by Moore McCormack. She departed New York on February 26th with a load of general cargo. In convoy at six to seven knots it took fifteen days to reach Trinidad. We bunkered and in twenty more days reached Rio de Janiero for discharge. We also discharged in Montevideo and Buenos Aires and loaded cases of canned meat for the military and the usual commercial cargoes, like coffee.

I got off in New York, got my Second Mate's license at the U.S. Maritime Service Upgrade School, and went as Second Mate on Mormac's Liberty Ship *Sherwood Anderson*.

From August 11 - 20th, we loaded at New York, Baltimore, Norfolk, and Newport News and on August 23rd, sailed in convoy for the Mediterranean. Destinations were always a secret, but we learned them from the stevedores or the cargo markings.

Forming a convoy took about twenty-four hours, but the ships were safely close to shore with good air cover. Ships were scheduled to sail every fifteen minutes. After a ship let the harbor pilot off, the escorts positioned her based on her number in the convoy. For example, 1010 would be the tenth ship in the tenth row of the convoy. Changing position in convoy was always dangerous because the Liberty had so little reserve power. It was easy to fall back, but difficult to move ahead or cross the lines of ships. I saw collisions, especially at night or when making emergency turns.

In fog each ship towed a fog buoy from the stern. The watch officer tried to keep the wake of the fog buoy of the ship ahead in sight by adjusting steering and speed. It was nerve wracking. A lot of people were scared thinking the wake was a submarine's periscope.

I stood my watch on the flying bridge, atop the bridge, so that I could see over the deck cargo. I was exposed to the elements and couldn't see through my binoculars in teeming rain. The Carpenter built me a shelter like a telephone booth.

Every day each Master flew flags signifying his noon position. They tried to wait until surrounding ships' flags went up in case their positions were wrong.

The *Sherwood Anderson* arrived Oran, Algiers seventeen days later. Submarines attacked the convoy, but I don't recall losing any ships. When a ship was hit, none of the other ships could stop. Seagoing tugs, stationed at the convoy's rear, attempted to rescue survivors.

After discharge at Oran and Nemours, we loaded for the invasion of southern France. In a small convoy we arrived at Toulon, France on D-Day plus three or four. The partly submerged, scuttled, fleet of French battleships, destroyers, and other vessels was a sad sight.

The *Anderson* was in a nest alongside a British Liberty Ship. Her officers invited us over for drinks. I had the obligatory shot of gin with a warm beer chaser and left. The Chief Mate continued drinking with the Brits. He came back very drunk, made insulting remarks, and swung at me. I knocked him cold with my three-cell flashlight and put him to bed with the help of a couple of ABs. We had an alcoholic on our hands.

Our next port was Marseilles, heavily damaged by the Germans. The ship's berth was along the inside of the Marseilles harbor breakwater. The Port Authority had us move away from the dock so divers could disarm a German bomb under our ship. We lay outside the breakwater for two days. The divers finally exploded it, without damage. I had plans to go out with some nurses from a hospital ship, but they left while we were anchored outside the breakwater.

In Oran, Nemours, and Marseilles the stevedores were Black U.S. Army Transportation Corps troops - hardworking, experienced, very good, proud men. Two men to a truck took turns driving and sleeping, working day and night to deliver gasoline and rations to Patton's Army. They haven't gotten the credit due them.

We picked up unexploded bombs and returned them to study why they didn't explode. By arrival at Charleston, South Carolina in convoy on December 10, 1944, the German submarine threat had been eliminated. In Charleston we took on fresh stores. I ate a raw onion for the first time. After Army rations, it tasted so good that I've loved onions ever since.

I went home for Christmas, got engaged to Natalie, and stayed in touch with Moore McCormack. It was strictly run, strong on the U.S. Naval Reserve, and had a high-quality port staff. I wanted to remain part of Mormac. The company had gone from thirty-eight ships in peacetime to 138 during World War II.

Captain Herman Mayo, the Marine Superintendent, always a gentleman and a friend of my father, asked me if I wanted to go on a ship to Murmansk in the northern Soviet Union. I replied that I did not want to go, but would, if needed. On February 1, 1945, he assigned me as Second Mate on the Liberty Ship *Benjamin Schlesinger*.

Sailing from New York on February 18, 1945, in convoy for Scotland, I found out why Captain Mayo wanted me. The Master was seventy-nine years old, tall, distinguished-looking, and an alcoholic incapacitated at sea. The Chief Mate, sixty-nine years old, hadn't been to sea in a long time and would not take charge on the bridge when the Captain could not.

In the Irish Sea abeam the Head of Kinsale in southern Ireland, I recalled that this was the area my grandfather fished and where the passenger liner *Lusitania* was sunk in World War I.

At the entrance to the Firth of Clyde in Scotland the convoy broke into single lines and waited for pilots. I called the Captain, but he was drunk, so I maneuvered a ship for the first time. The Pilot came aboard and asked for the Captain. I said that he was indisposed. We anchored safely on March 4, 1945.

I went touring in Glasgow. The Captain had drunk two cases of whiskey kept aboard for medicinal purposes, and resupplied. Winds were strong, so both anchors were down.

On March 12, 1945, we sailed, destination either Murmansk or Archangel, via the Minch off northwest Scotland. The drunken Captain locked the charts in his safe. When I couldn't see the ship in front of us, I followed the buoys I could see. The convoy was escorted by two British baby carriers, heavy cruisers, anti-aircraft cruisers, destroyers, corvettes, and three or four North Sea trawlers behind the convoy to pick up survivors and deliver them to the cruisers or destroyers.

Luftwaffe, four-engine, high-altitude bombers and JU 88 twin-engine, fighter-bombers used as torpedo planes, flew low across the lines of the convoy at least once a day, and hit the most available target. The British cargo ships carried Hurricanes to catapult off their bows to fight the Luftwaffe. If they had enough gasoline left, the British pilots flew to England. If not, they parachuted into the sea.

In darkness German submarines attacked with their conning towers out of the water and used their diesel power to get inside the escorts. We were happy to see stormy weather so the bombers couldn't fly, and the submarines couldn't operate. Twenty-four-hour darkness did made it difficult for the Germans to find us.

Constant snow and sleet in sub-zero temperatures made for sea ice on the ship and its rigging. The Navy issued us special clothing - two sets of heavy woolen underwear, three pairs of heavy woolen socks, woolen gloves with leather mittens, aviator caps with ear flaps, goggles, British balaclavas with openings for the eyes and nose, blue wool trousers like overalls, a hooded, waterproof duffel coat, and felt boots with rubber overshoes. I was also issued a rubber escape suit with a built-in life preserver, but putting it on took fifteen minutes.

Sea watches were the usual four hours on and eight off, but General Quarters for battle stations was called frequently. I averaged two to four hours' sleep a day, without removing my clothes and ready to get out quickly, like a fireman. I didn't shave and even rushed my toilet stops due to the danger of being hit. The Germans aimed their first torpedo at the Liberty's engine room, so that it also hit in or under the living quarters and also destroyed the two lifeboats on that side. If the engine room crew had been killed, the screw kept turning until seawater reached the boilers because there was no one to shut down the plant. Life rafts, stored forward and aft, were released into the water, but the ship continued steaming past them. In a wet raft or in the water you would die of hypothermia in twenty minutes.

On a Liberty one lifeboat on each side was motorized. Training on them took place on smooth seas in port, but at sea they were difficult to launch. I think that the biggest cause of deaths was damaged lifeboats or capsizing during launching.

Losses were classified, but to my recollection, we lost five to seven cargo ships, no tankers or ammunition ships because I didn't see any big explosions or fires.

A Russian escort met us two days out from Murmansk. On March 19, 1945, the convoy went from ten columns to one entering the Kola Inlet to the Kola River. Sometimes, submarines submerged on both sides of the inlet fired at the sounds of entering ships until all their torpedoes were gone. The Captain was drunk, and the Chief Mate was sick, so I was in change. There were no pilots. I had to dodge sunken ships. My friends, the Chief Engineer and the Gunnery Officer, were my witnesses whenever I exceeded my authority as Second Mate like this. I was in a squall abeam a Norwegian tanker and pulled ahead. A torpedo hit the tanker, and the noise brought my Captain to the bridge. He loudly criticizing me for passing the tanker too close then went below, and I didn't see him again for two days.

A pilot boarded and took us to an anchorage. We doubled the Gun Crew watches. Murmansk's buildings had been destroyed by constant German air attacks and replaced by log huts.

The *Benjamin Schlesinger's* deck cargo of locomotives got us priority docking. The crew gave gifts of perfume and lipstick to the female stevedores. They were no beauties. It was impossible to tell how much of their dress was clothes and how much was fat.

Each crewmember received 1,000 rubles and had to return what he didn't spend. I bought two bottles of perfume for my fiance, two packs of tea, and a bottle of vodka at the Intourist Hotel. There was nothing else to buy.

To celebrate the convoy's arrival the Soviets invited each Captain, Chief Engineer, and Gunnery Officer to a banquet. Our Captain said that he was sick, and the Chief Mate didn't want to go, so I went, dressed in the Captain's uniform. As the youngest Captain in the convoy, I got a seat of honor next to the Soviet translator. He had stainless steel false teeth. We ate ten sumptuous courses, including caviar. After each of many toasts to Roosevelt, Churchill, and Stalin, we held our empty glasses upside down over our heads. I survived by substituting water for vodka. The Soviets drove us back to our ships by jeep so that none of us fell in the snow and froze to death.

The Chart Room on Liberties had a Scott radio, which couldn't be intercepted by submarines. I rigged a speaker in my cabin and enjoyed British Broadcasting Company news and shows. In Murmansk we got the news of President Roosevelt's death. It was a heavy blow to all.

After discharging the locomotives, we returned to the river. There were no boats, so we couldn't go ashore. Six to eight of us played bridge almost constantly. No money was involved, but there was a lot of arguing.

The Soviet stevedores were very good at discharging cargo, and there was no theft. We sailed on April 29, 1945, after forty days in Murmansk discharging and waiting for an inbound convoy's escorts to take us out. Supposedly, outbound convoys were not attacked, but outside the Kola Inlet I saw British destroyers sink or ram three German submarines in surface action. En route back to Scotland, submarines attacked the convoy, but there were no losses.

We anchored in the Clyde on May 8, 1945, the day the war in Europe ended. Since we got no answer to our blinker light request for a liberty boat, I made the six-mile trip to Glasgow in our motor lifeboat, towing another lifeboat load of crewmembers. The Captain was displeased, but I told him I'd bring him back some liquor.

As the Ship's Doctor, I had access to the ship's liquor supply. I poured two bottles of whiskey into several medicine bottles and also brought cigars and cigarettes ashore with me. I was enjoying myself, smoking a cigar and gave another to a Scot who asked for one. The pubs closed for fear of over-crowding.

I bought a male Scotch terrier from a breeder. One crewman bought the runt of the litter, and another bought a female. The three of us went to the movies with the dogs under our coats, and they yipped throughout the show.

On May 12, 1945, we sailed, in convoy due to rogue German submarines. Off New York we were sent to the Delaware Capes.

I told the Third Mate that at about 10 P.M. on his watch, he would sight a sea buoy and then board the Delaware Pilot. When I came on watch at midnight, I asked where the pilot was. The Third Mate replied that the

Captain, drunk, would not permit a course change at the sea buoy, so the *Benjamin Schlesinger* continued south. With soundings becoming shallower, I called the Chief Engineer and Gunnery Officer to the bridge to observe my exercise of authority. The ship lurched. We passed a flashing green light on a buoy marked "FIS." Since our whereabouts were unknown, I anchored and checked the charts. "FIS" was Fenwick Island Shoal off the Delaware coast. Passing over the shoal had caused the ship to lurch.

When the Chief Mate came on watch at 4 A.M., I told him to wait at anchor until daylight. The Captain asked where we were. I replied that fog had set in, and we had to anchor. We proceeded up the Delaware River and through the Chesapeake and Delaware Canal to Baltimore without further incident. I was relieved and took my dog on the train to Boston. Natalie and I got married on June 13, 1945. After our honeymoon, I went to a thirty-day USMS Upgrade School and got my Chief Mate's license.

On August 13, 1945, I reported to Moore McCormack in New York for a ship. Japan surrendered on August 15th. On August 24th, I was assigned to the Liberty Ship *Robert Rogers* as Chief Officer and sailed on September 12, 1945, to Norfolk for lay-up. I returned to Boston by train, carrying two twenty-five-pound bags of sugar and a ship's clock.

On October 2, 1945, I reported to the *SS Studding Sail*, a C1MAV1, called a Cimavi, at the U.S. Navy Seabee Base at Davidsonville, Rhode Island. The C1MAV1 was the only dry cargo ship built with the engine aft during World War II. We sailed for Okinawa on October 20, 1945 with a load of heavy steel.

Navigation lights were still out in the Caribbean, so we held to wide passages between the islands.

We cleared the Panama Canal on October 30, 1945, on a Great Circle route for Okinawa at nine knots. About four days out, the Chief Engineer announced that the ship didn't carry enough fresh water, nor could we make enough, to get to Okinawa. We were directed to San Pedro, California, where I was transferred off the ship.

Admiral Bauman:

In 1944 I joined the Liberty Ship *Joseph R. Lamar* as Third Mate. We took a load of bombs to Milford Haven, England. I made two trips on her and on one passed my first ship, the Liberty Ship *Stephen C. Foster.* Steaming in convoy was difficult for some Deck Officers used to sailing alone, but I had grown up with it from my first trip as Third Mate.

Our Captain, who was in his late twenties, used a small scale chart entering Southampton, England.   After dropping anchor, he noticed on a large-scale chart that we were in the area of a submerged pipeline.   Getting underway the next day, our anchor windlass stopped because PLUTO, the six-inch PipeLine Under The Ocean to carry oil for the invasion of France, was on an anchor fluke. Using hawsers, we disengaged PLUTO.

During World War II, only six months' sea time, not the usual twelve, was necessary to sit for the next higher license. I used all my spare time to study for the Second Mate's examination and passed it without going to any prep school.

To get the Mediterranean Middle East combat ribbon, I got on the *SS Felipe de Neve*, a Liberty troop ship going to the Mediterranean. As thousands of Liberty Ships were launched, they became desperate for names. She was named after the first Governor of California, Philip of the Snow. It was always difficult to communicate our name by blinker light. The then-new radar was installed on this ship.

Felipe de Neve could carry 1,000 troops or prisoners in summer and 600 in winter. On V-E Day, because a guard became ill, we were in Gibraltar with 1,000 German POWs loaded in Marseilles for the U.S. We were ordered to rendezvous with a U.S.-bound convoy, but missed it, so proceeded to the Azores for supplies. When the prisoners noticed the morning sun to starboard, not astern, they asked where we were going. I jokingly replied, "Russia." The Captain cautioned me that my joke could cause a riot.

A guard said that he heard a female was among the prisoners. The Captain had all 1,000 of them strip for salt water showers from the ship's hoses. No female was found. We returned the POWs to Marseilles and embarked 1,000 American troops for Newport News, Virginia.

Captain Schindler:

In 1962, during the U.S. Naval blockade of Cuba, U.S. destroyers asked questions like the ship's name, nationality and cargo by blinker light. The Captain of the T-2 tanker *SS Mission Buenaventura* ordered me, as Third Mate, to reply, "None of your business." I thought it ill advised to offend a warship with guns trained on us, so to every question I blinked that we were an American ship on the high seas.

When I was Chief Mate on another T-2, the *SS Henry*, we cleared the Suez Canal northbound the day before the 1967 Six-Day War. Egyptian truck convoys were lining up alongside the canal. A day later and we would have been caught when the canal was closed.

Captain Glen:

American Export Lines' Far East run was Japan, Korea, Hong Kong, Manila, Okinawa and occasionally, Vietnam. Cargo for Vietnam usually went to staging areas in the Philippines or Okinawa to minimize the number of ships sitting in the war zone. I had friends on United Fruit Company's reefer ships sitting in the war zone as warehouses full of refrigerated military cargoes.

In 1974-1975, I spent six months as Second Mate on the *SS Admiral William M. Callaghan*, about 750 feet long and powered by twin gas turbines. She was operated by Sunexport, a wholly owned subsidiary of AEL, and Sun Shipbuilding Corporation, its builder, and was under charter to the military. The U.S. Army was in charge of her cargo and the U.S. Navy her routing. We ran to Bremerhaven, Germany and then to Israel, supplying the Israelis with tanks, armored personnel carriers, and ammunition.

One stormy night in the eastern Mediterranean, we got a distress call from a Cypriot fishing vessel going down. We responded with our position. A Russian ship gave a position further away and was slower than our ship. Our Radio Operator found that the call sign of the fishing vessel did not match its name. As we homed in on her by radar and Radio Direction Finder, we found a discrepancy in the position she gave and a second target. The second target turned out to be the Russian ship. The Captain and I discussed the discrepancies, our load of 300 tanks plus ammunition, and being under secret orders in the eastern Mediterranean, one of the world's hot spots, and decided to leave the area under cover of darkness.

The *Callaghan* was a high-tech ship, even carried a spare engine, which could be installed in six to eight hours. Her two 120-ton booms could be married to give enormous heavy-lift capacity for cargoes such as landing craft. Vehicles could be driven on and off via roll on - roll off decks equipped with special ventilating and fire-fighting systems. She was fast, but burned a tremendous amount of fuel and was put in lay-up. The *Callaghan* was activated from lay-up in Baltimore in 1990, for Operation Desert Shield.

Captain Smeenk:

My first experience as a ship's only Third Mate was in 1969, on Marine Transport Lines' *SS Hobart Victory* bound for Saigon, South Vietnam with military cargo. Usually the Chief Mate is a day-worker, supervising cargo stowage and ship's maintenance and doing paperwork. Due to a shortage of officers during the Vietnam war, the Chief Mate had to also stand bridge watches. We earned 100% of wages as a war bonus. At anchor in the Saigon River a couple of shells fell around us, adding another $300 to my pay.

Ships like the *Hobart Victory* were built about 1943 and laid-up at the end of World War II. In lay-up they were not dehumidified, which caused engine problems, breakdowns, and eventual towing of some of them when they were broken-out for Vietnam. The rotor on the main turbine of the *Hobart Victory* had sagged, so the power plant required above-average maintenance.

Captain Wanner:

About 1969, I sailed into Vietnam on a new U.S. Lines ship, the *SS American Racer*, which had a large reefer capacity. In two-month round trips we carried thousands of tons of frozen beef for the troops.

In Operation Desert Storm it appeared to me that the most valuable ship was the ro-ro, where heavy-lift cargoes, like tanks, could be loaded or discharged via ramps and be ready for the field in twelve hours.

Mr. Bullock:

Finally, MEBA II came through for me. For a $2,000-initiation fee and $1,000 annual dues, I went as Third Mate on the USNS *Capella* in November 1988. She was a big SL7 container ship, about 42,00 gross tons, 980 feet long, and capable of thirty-five knots with twin screws. She had been inefficient in Sealand's container trade, so was sold to the Federal Maritime Administration, then to the U.S. Navy. Four SL7s were pre-positioned in reserve operational status at military terminals in the U.S. They sailed once a year to shipyards for overhaul and for occasional military exercises. Military vehicles rolled on and off. Three jumbo booms and cranes made *Capella* self-sustaining in loading and discharging.

After blowing a high-pressure steam line on sea trials, we were anchoring in Chesapeake Bay. Our lack of propulsion on one propeller caused the ship to collide with the bow of another pre-positioned ship, the *SS Duane T. Williams*. The Capella was left with an eight by ten-foot hole in her port side.

I was Second Mate on the *Capella*, when she was the first U.S. Sealift ship to reach Saudi Arabia in 1990, in support of Operation Desert Shield. In fourteen days we carried 150 members of the 24th (Mechanized) Infantry Division, of Fort Stuart, Georgia, with their tanks, trucks, and missiles, from Garden City, Georgia to Daman, Saudi Arabia. At thirty-three knots, *Capella* crossed the Atlantic in four and a half days burning a barrel of oil a minute. As ships were broken-out of lay-up for this operation, crewmembers were hard to find. We had about fifteen World War II veterans in their late-sixties. The Radio Operator was eighty-five years old.

For fear of mines, U.S. Navy ships escorted the *Capella* through the Straits of Hormuz into the Persian Gulf. A flotilla of Iranian boats with fifty caliber machine guns circled the ship. We discharged our cargo in five days.

UNITED STATES NAVAL RESERVE (USNR)

Captain Carter:

In 1930 I joined the USNR as an Ensign with the promise that I would be promoted along with officers on active duty. When I was called to active duty in 1943, I was still an Ensign. On sixteen days' notice, I reported to Norfolk for general deck duties on a Navy ship under construction. A brand new Chief Mate was the Executive Officer. The Captain made me the Navigator, but could not promote or release me.

My civilian employer, The Board of Underwriters, convinced the Navy to discharge me in favor of working at the ammunition loading facility in Baltimore. I spent the rest of the war in this very efficient operation.

Commodore Alexanderson:

In December 1939 the Navy wanted thirty-five Merchant Marine Reserve officers for one year's active duty on fleet support ships. I was commissioned in the USNR in 1932, and was a Lieutenant. Captain Schuyler Cummings, United States Lines' Marine Superintendent, told me that it would of value to the company if I volunteered. Within a week, I had orders to the *USS Melville*, a destroyer tender in San Diego.

Just before Christmas, I got a driver's license and drove across country with my wife, Dot, her mother, and our two children.

As the first reserve officer going to an all-Regular Navy ship, I got a cold reception at the San Diego Naval District Headquarters. But I was well received by the *Melville's* Executive Officer, Commander Hopwood, who later became Commander of the Pacific Fleet. The *Melville* was destined for Pearl Harbor to service destroyers, so I sent my family back home to Brooklyn.

Halfway into my year of active duty, the Navy wrote that they were pleased with my service, and I would remain "for the duration." My seniority at U.S. Lines would continue. The duration turned out to be six and three quarter years for me.

I was Navigator on the *Melville* in Norfolk for overhaul, when Pearl Harbor was attacked. We proceeded to Londonderry, Northern Ireland to overhaul fifty old destroyers the U.S. gave the British, and to anchor off Iceland to service merchant ships going to Murmansk, Soviet Union.

In 1942 and 1943, *Melville* supported the Atlantic Fleet and was also a flagship. By this time, I was a Lieutenant Commander and the *Melville's* Executive Officer.

In early 1944, I was ordered to take command of the *USS Livingston* (AP 163,) a Liberty Ship converted to a troop transport. After a year out of the U.S., I spent a couple of days with my family in New York en route to join the *Livingston* in San Francisco.

My officers were all young. Only two had experience: the Executive Officer, who had been with me at U.S. Lines, and the Navigator, a Naval Academy graduate, assigned after some kind of personal trouble.

We carried 1,500 U.S. Navy Seabees and landing craft on deck to the South Pacific. The Seabees built me a plywood wheelhouse over the bridge.

We carried troops in the invasion of Saipan. A Japanese torpedo plane dropped its load so low that it went under us, and the pilot nearly fetched up in our mast.

As a Commander, I was ordered to take command of the *USS Gage* (APA 136,) a Victory-type attack transport. I flew from the South Pacific to New York. We again drove to San Diego, then to Seattle, and Astoria, Oregon, where the ship was commissioned. On Thanksgiving Day, 1944, we sailed. My pregnant wife got as far as Cincinnati, where her gasoline coupons ran out. A friend in the Army got her enough coupons for the drive back to Brooklyn.

We carried 1,500 medical personnel to Tulagi and Guadalcanal. Units of the Sixth Marines embarked. After training exercises, *Gage* participated in the original landings at Okinawa on Easter Sunday morning, 1945, and took 400 wounded to a hospital on Saipan.

I carried troops to San Francisco and Seattle, where I was relieved by Elliott Midgett, who'd been with me at U.S. Lines. When I arrived home in September 1945, my four-year-old son, John, told me he had a new baby sister, Linda, three months old.

My Navy Detailer, Stanley Thompson, Executive Officer when I was Third Mate in the passenger ship *SS California*, sent me to Norfolk as Commanding Officer of the troop ship *USS General Leroy Eltinge* (AP 154).

Going out light through the Mediterranean and Suez Canal, *Eltinge* picked up a full load, 400 officers and 2,800 enlisted men, in Karachi. These Army Air Forces men spent the war flying "over the hump" in the China Burma India Theater. They were wound up as tight as a drum during the voyage. They disembarked in Hoboken, New Jersey in time for Christmas, 1945.

Before Christmas, *Eltinge* sailed for Shanghai. Among the few passengers was John Hersey, going to do research for his book *Hiroshima*. On New Year's Day, 1946, we began loading passengers, Army fliers, troops, a U.S. Marine detachment, civilian internees, Catholic nuns and priests, Red Cross girls, and Army and Navy nurses. Some passengers were mentally ill, a few so sick that they had to be put off in Manila. I soon put a stop to fraternization among the passengers, causing an Army nurse to say on arrival in Seattle, "We may not have had good morale, but we sure had good morals."

We carried replacement troops to Inchon, Korea. In San Diego the Captain and part of the crew of the German pocket cruiser *Prince Eugen*, seized as war reparations, embarked for New York and transport back to Germany. The goal of the pleasant Captain was to immigrate to the U.S.

The *Eltinge* was turned over to the Army Transport Command in May 1946. In September, I returned to U.S. Lines, almost seven years after my one year of active duty.

As Captain, USNR, I was one of six U.S. Lines officers who conducted sea trials of the aircraft carrier *USS Forrestal* from July to September 1955. I was promoted to Rear Admiral, USNR, on October 1, 1959.

Captain Fowler:

When Pearl Harbor was bombed on December 7, 1941, I was an Ensign in the Naval Reserve. I decided that I would rather serve in the Merchant Marine. On December 8 th, I quit my job at Sparrows Point Shipyard in Baltimore and on December 9 th, was reinstated in the Masters Mates and Pilots union.

Captain Sulzer:

In 1982, the Navy asked me, as a Reserve Lieutenant, to set up the Department of Naval Science at the Great Lakes Maritime Academy, Travis City, Michigan. I continued on active duty until May 1984, working on a Navy project in Newport, Rhode Island and then writing the training program for the Navy's Merchant Marine Reserve Program.

I've regularly performed active duty for training and am now a Captain, USNR, Merchant Marine Reserve.

HEAVY WEATHER

Commodore Alexanderson:

Avoiding bad weather was always a concern for masters of passenger ships in North Atlantic service. The northernmost track, Track C, was the most economical, but the weather could be rough. Tracks B and A were more southerly alternatives for better weather. Because I always pursued the best possible weather, in all my years at sea I never saw an iceberg.

Captain Atkinson:

On a trip to Rotterdam with coal the *SS William R. Lewis* met Force 9 winds. A heavy sea boarded on the port side amidships on January 12, 1946. The wave carried away the accommodation ladder, the Number 2 lifeboat, a door in the bulwark, the reels for the lifeboat falls, and the box of life preservers. It stove in the kick-out panel in the door to the officers' quarters, and flooded their rooms. My letter to Black Diamond's Marine Superintendent stated that, aside from the damage and losing a day and a half to fog in the English Channel, the trip was quite uneventful.

As Master I went through several hurricanes with the usual damage. I'm a fair-weather sailor and believe in avoiding bad weather or slowing down to the point where I could ride easily. I always told the company that it was better to be a couple of days late than to spend a couple of weeks in the shipyard for repairs.

Captain Fowler:

As Master of the *SS Casimir Pulaski* taking coal from Newport News to St. Nazaire, France I encountered very heavy weather from January 11-29, 1948. My log shows winds up to Force 9 and being hove to in mountainous seas. The chain locker was flooded, portholes cracked, and the lifeboats were damaged.

Later in 1948, as Master of the *SS Thomas R. Marshall*, I was just south of the Azores inbound from Europe in ballast. A hurricane due south of us was traveling west at almost our speed of twelve knots. It then curved to the east-northeast at fifteen to twenty knots and hit us with east southeast winds. I changed course more to the northwest to keep the eye south of us.

By 6 A.M. the wind was increasing with no change in direction. The barometer was falling rapidly, rainsqualls were coming in, and visibility was very bad. About 11 A.M. we ran into the eye, or, rather, the eye ran into us. The roar of the wind was so loud that I could not hear the Third Mate talking to me in the wheelhouse. The seas were confused and rough, but I was able to turn the ship around to put the wind on my quarter. The center of the hurricane's eye came over us. There was no wind and the sky was clear, but the horizon was black. The ship's rigging was covered with birds taking refuge in the eye.

The Radio Operator brought me a message from the agent in Norfolk requesting my ETA. I had Sparks reply, "Presently hove to in eye of hurricane. Will advise later."

At noon the hurricane passed over. By 2 P.M. the winds had moderated considerably, and we were back on course. We arrived Norfolk without any damage.

On a later voyage to Cherbourg, fog set in just as we entered the English Channel. The *Marshall* had radar since she was a troopship in World War II. I used it to get her to anchor just off the Cherbourg breakwater. A reporter from *The Cherbourg Press* interviewed me about the use of radar. The agent gave me a copy of the lengthy article he wrote in the December 2, 1948 edition about the wonders of radar. I could only make out the ship's name and mine. Many years later, after I retired, my niece translated this article for me.

I was Chief Mate on the *SS* American Oriole in 1951, carrying about 3,500 tons of general cargo from Antwerp for New York, when I experienced the worst weather of my sea-going career.

After we departed the English Channel, Force 7 to 9 winds came from the southwest, west, and then northeast. Very heavy seas developed. Halfway across the Atlantic it became apparent that, if conditions did not improve, we would not have enough bunkers to reach New York, but could possibly make St. Johns, Newfoundland.

One morning, the steering gear on the bridge was not responding properly. While engineers worked on correcting the problem, I took over steering from the after steering station on the raised poop deck. The Bosun and Deck Maintenance AB held onto the railing around the steering station and faced aft away from the wind. I did not bother trying to keep my eyes on the magnetic compass, just keeping the vessel headed into the heavy seas was enough. As the bow started down into an incoming wave, I could look over the top of the forward masts at the top of the wave. I have no idea how high the seas were, but they were very frightening. The Bosun fell when the ship went down into the trough of a wave, but he and the AB were able to hold onto me. A wave over the stern left me knee-deep in water, but quickly washed over the side as we started up an incoming wave. The steering gear problem was corrected, and we changed back to steering from the lower wheelhouse.

About 2 A.M. the ship fell into the trough of a wave and took it over the port side. I jumped from my bunk into water up to my knees. The wave washed away the door from the boat deck, letting the sea go through the passageway to my side.

The Captain decided to turn the ship around because another wave like that one would probably be our last. We were in a trough with the bow pointed a little off to starboard. Captain Peter J. Frantzen ordered the helmsman to put the wheel hard right. The ship came around in a few minutes, and the seas were then on our quarter. With increased speed we were able to ride the incoming seas fairly well.

In the morning I checked the damage. Both port lifeboats were smashed. The forward boat had hit the engineers' rooms. The after boat was on the Engine Room Hatch. I had the Bosun salvage gear from the boats, puncture their air tanks so that they would sink, and shove them over the side.

We proceeded south to the Azores for bunkers. The ship was surveyed and received a Certificate of Seaworthiness. After arrival in New York, we learned that the storm damaged several large passenger vessels and made them late in arriving.

Captain McCarthy:

I joined the *SS Mooremacdale* as Chief Mate on August 25, 1948, sailed from New York for Brazil on August 30 th, and met a hurricane on August 31st. The tarpaulins covering Number 3 hatch blew away. In heavy rollers I went out with the Deck Crew to put two tarps on. To put the wind on the stern, the Captain ordered full ahead and hard left, then stopped engines, to get through the troughs in the seas and get a lee. The wind blew the dirt in the tarps all over us and ripped my shirt off. We secured the first tarp on the hatch and then the second one over it.

The Captain gave the crew and the officers bottles of whiskey to celebrate completing the difficult job. The twelve passengers, including some missionaries, looked at me, no shirt and covered with dirt, like I was a pirate.

Admiral Bauman:

During the war, ships always carried deck cargoes. The winters of 1944 and 1945 were particularly severe in the North Atlantic. In 1944 we loaded 8,000 tons of bombs in the holds and tanks and trucks on deck on the Liberty Ship *Stephen C. Foster*. Our crossing was completed safely, but on a later voyage, a deck cargo of gliders was lost to a storm. All that remained on the deck were two wheels.

Captain Schindler:

In 1963, I joined the 15,000-ton *SS Solomon B. Thurman*, an ugly looking thing built a year before for Lykes Brothers Steamship Company. We loaded general cargo in the U.S. Gulf for northern Europe. In the middle of the North Atlantic in winter we were in a storm with ninety-knot winds. Our height of eye on the bridge was usually fifty feet above the water. These waves were at bridge level. Forty-eight turnbuckles on Army tanks in the tween decks broke loose, but the crew secured them without one tank breaking loose.

Captain Smeenk:

About 1970, off Cape Hatteras, North Carolina I experienced the worst weather of my career, Force 10 winds and thirty-foot seas. The radar antenna could not turn because of the force of the wind.

On my runs to Northern Europe pilots boarded Lykes' container ships using launches from large mother ships off Antwerp, Rotterdam, and Bremerhaven. In really bad weather the Pilot, wearing a wet suit, is lowered from a helicopter onto a wing of the bridge, the stern, or focsle. In Rotterdam a small helicopter landed on a hatch on the open foredeck of a Lykes ship. Helicopters lower pilots onto very large tankers and containerships fifty miles at sea.

Since the late-1960s, American ships transiting the English Channel and North Sea pick-up North Sea Pilots. They stand watches like the ship's officers. Masters of

European ships are familiar enough with these waters to pilot their own ships.

I dealt with three hurricanes in a row in the summer of 1996, as Second mate on the *SS Nuevo San Juan*, a former U.S. Lines Lancer class container ship, shuttling between Port Elizabeth, New Jersey; San Juan, Puerto Rico; Jacksonville, Florida; San Juan, and Port Elizabeth. We avoided the worst of Hurricane Bertha three times. Proceeding from Port Elizabeth to San Juan on July 8 - 9, we stayed about 150 miles north and east of Bertha's track. Steaming north from San Juan we got swells and winds about Force 7 off the Carolinas. By the time we docked in Port Elizabeth, Bertha was overhead as rain and Force 6 winds. Working cargo stopped only when the wind exceeded thirty-five knots, because we couldn't position the containers.

To avoid Hurricane Eduardo, we found beautiful weather and added only six hours by steaming south through the Old Bahama Channel and the Straits of Florida.

Southbound, we hove-to from September 9 th to the 10th, off the north coast of Puerto Rico in heavy rains and Force 8 winds with occasional higher gusts, until Hurricane Hortense's eye passed south of Puerto Rico and 200 miles from the *Nuevo San Juan*. After discharging and loading, we departed San Juan on September 14th, and slowly steamed north in fifteen to twenty-foot seas in the safe southeast semicircle. Letting Hortense pass cost one and half days.

Captain Wanner:

On my last trip as Captain of United States Lines' *SS American Lark*, I left Yokohama, Japan for California in February 1986. Steering east-southeast, we got caught in a very heavy winter storm moving from the northwest.

I made the unwise decision to try to outrun the storm by putting the wind and sea at my stern. For the first

126

twenty four hours it seemed like a pretty good idea. The following day, the seas built to the point that I had to reduce speed to avoid driving the bow under when the storm, seas and wind were on the stern. There was no possible way to turn the ship. She would have capsized.

I slowed down to eighty revolutions per minute, which avoided taking green seas over the bow. When I slowed to seventy revolutions, I took green seas over the stern. They flooded the aft compartments, paint lockers, and steering gear flats. I put her back to eighty revolutions and made a balance between green water over the bow and over the stern.

We were rolling thirty-five degrees to port and starboard with containers stacked five high on deck. At the beginning of the voyage the lashings over the containers were tight. When it was over, the lashings over the top tier of containers had two feet of slack, but we didn't lose one container.

The starboard running light was knocked off. When I requisitioned a new one in California, the Port Captain said that he went to sea for a lot of years and never saw anyone steam a running light off.

I've been through the eye of a hurricane and the usual heavy weather, but this was the worst weather I've seen.

Mr. Bullock:

The MV *Lawrence Gianella*, a T-5 tanker built in 1985 without a raised bow, did not take seas like older ships. The Captain diligently tried to avoid heavy weather.

I was Second Mate on the *MV Green Lake* from January through June 1999, in one storm after another carrying Toyotas from Japan. The Captain said that they were the worst Pacific storms he'd seen. But not one of the 5000 Toyotas aboard got even a scratch.

CASUALTIES

On September 8, 1934, the Ward Line's luxury liner *SS Morrow Castle*, en route from Havana, Cuba to New York, burned off the New Jersey Coast with a loss of 135 passengers and crew.

Captain Carter:

Sailing south from New York one night, we passed the *SS Morrow Castle* with all her lights on. We later learned that she was attempting to fight a fire without knowing how bad it actually was.

Captain Atkinson:

On June 21, 1972, I paid-off as Master on the *ST Western Hunter* in Karachi. The Chief Engineer came back from vacation and went into the after peak tank with a shore contractor. When the contractor's son came aboard to see his father, we went looking for the two of them. The Chief Engineer found his relieving Chief Engineer and the Pakistani contractor in the tank, both dead from lack of oxygen. He also passed out and had to be pulled out of the tank by the line around him. The First Assistant Engineer went into the tank wearing an oxygen breathing apparatus and brought out the two bodies.

Captain Fowler:

I was Master of the *SS Thomas R. Marshall* returning from Italy in 1948. About 8 P.M. on a calm night halfway across the Atlantic, the ship vibrated terribly. By the time I ran to the pilot house, everything was quiet. All that the Chief Engineer and myself saw where the propeller should have been was the rusty, broken shaft.

I sent a message to the operators and the next day was advised that the *SS Foundation Lillian*, a Canadian deep sea tug based in Bermuda, was on its way to pick us up. The tug instructed us by radio to slack off the anchor chain using the Number 1 cargo boom, and heave the anchor onto the *Marshall's* deck. After unshipping the anchor, we put a length of line onto the end of the anchor chain, ready to pass to the tug.

Waiting in fine weather for a tug to arrive, we drifted about 25 miles a day in a northeast direction. The crew caught a mako shark using a meat hook with a big piece of bacon on a heaving line. Trying to bring it aboard, the Third Mate shot the shark five times with my revolver, but it broke free.

Four days later, with the weather still good, the tug arrived. Her crew got our manila line aboard with some difficulty and attached the tug's towing hawser to our anchor chain. We slacked out fifteen fathoms of chain, secured it with the devil's claw and wired it to the forward bitts. After twelve uneventful days under tow, tugs met us at Hampton Roads, Virginia for dry-docking.

Mr. Ramsey:

In 1962 I was Third Mate on American Export Lines' *SS Express*, when a cargo of jute caught fire in Madras, India. We fought it by pouring water into the forward cargo holds. On the second day of fire fighting, the ship rolled fifteen degrees toward the dock from the weight of the water in the holds. Our National Maritime Union crew jumped either ashore or overboard. The Purser and the Chief Steward tried to launch the offshore lifeboat. The officers fought the fire in six-hour shifts for ten days. All but three crewmembers stayed uptown in hotels. The fire knocked out electrical power forward, so back in the U.S. the water-damaged cargo was discharged using shore cranes. The ship went into a Wehauken, New Jersey shipyard for repairs.

On my next Export Line ship, the *SS Flying Gull*, with the author as the other Third Mate, the most eventful part of an around-the-world voyage was a collision with a new Greek ore carrier, the *SS Batus*, in 1963. Leaving the harbor in Kobe, Japan, I was on watch, relieving Second Mate Leo Valentius for supper. The *Gull* had the right of way. Instead of a half astern bell, the *Batus* got a half ahead bell on her turbo electric engine and headed for us. Captain John McLean took the conn from the pilot and almost succeeded in turning the *Gull* away. *Batus* hit us on the port side of Number 1 Hatch above the water line and pushed us over about fifteen degrees. She missed a Mercedes stowed in the upper tween deck by a few feet. The Chief Mate and the Bosun were standing by the anchor and ran back from the bow to avoid being hit. It took a week in a Kobe shipyard to repair the hole in the port bow.

Captain Schindler:

I loaded grain at Port Arthur, Texas in 1967, as Chief Mate on the *SS Henry.* My wife, Pat, joined me. We proceeded toward the Suez Canal because it was expected to reopen soon. No such luck. The canal remained closed for years. We then needed enough fuel to go around the Cape of Good Hope, so took on bunkers in Freetown, Sierra Leone and Durban, South Africa. After discharging our cargo in Bombay, we loaded oil in Bahrain and the Trucal States of Abu Dahbi, and bunkered in Mombassa, Kenya; Capetown, South Africa, and St. Vincent's in the Cape Verde Islands.

About thirty miles outside Funchal, Madeira, bound for Antwerp, Belgium, I heard a thud. From the midship house I saw the aft half of the ship bending up and down. I thought that she broken her back. Instead, one of the propeller's four blades had fallen off.

The company was not the least bit excited. The owner did not arrive in Funchal for a few weeks. I later learned that when the propeller broke, the freight was "at risk." Under the terms of the insurance this meant that, if for any reason the cargo was not delivered, the insurer paid the carrier the freight. Freight rates were very high at the time. The voyage was declared abandoned because the ship could not sail, and the owner was paid $3,000,000 freight.

After a tow to Lisbon, Portugal, the ship's hull insurance paid for repair of the propeller, which also gave the owner a free dry-docking.

Pat expected a routine three-month voyage from Port Arthur to Bombay and back. Instead, she visited Africa, Europe, the Middle East, and Asia and had a lovely month in Madeira on a trip that lasted six months and one day.

About 1977, the *SS American Hawk* collided with the sailboat *Miracle of God* being operated by two Cubans in the Straits of Florida. At dusk in a crossing situation we blew our whistle and changed course. The sailboat turned into us. I was working on deck and saw only his mast as he bounced along the ship's side. I prepared the lifeboat for launching, but he left the scene. We called the Coast Guard. A cutter intercepted him and charged him with failure to obey the Rules of the Road. I think that it's a miracle that the *Miracle of God* stayed afloat after being hit by a 33,000-ton tanker.

I briefly sailed as Master of Alton Steamship Company's *SS Flor* and in 1978, transferred to their *SS Port* at Pensacola, Florida. The *Port* was a good ship, a converted C-4, formerly owned by Calmar Steamship Company. She had three 105-foot hatches forward and a smaller hatch aft of the house, all with hydraulic hatch covers, and two, big whirly cranes.

Halfway across the Gulf of Mexico, bound for Houston, the Bosun smelled smoke. Because the cargo was bagged flour stacked to the overhead, we could not locate the fire. I decided not to open Number 2 hatch and tried to smother the fire with the ship's carbon dioxide fire fighting system. We headed for Galveston at maximum speed, but the Coast Guard would not let me dock. I had to anchor in choppy water with forty two men and two wives aboard and no more carbon dioxide.

I did not believe that the fire was out and spent several days asking for assistance. The Galveston Fire Department came out, cut a hole in the deck, and put out the fire. In a week, it had burned like charcoal, leaving a four by four-foot hole in bagged flour and cracking twenty feet of the ship's deck by its intense heat.

We discharged the damaged cargo, had the crack repaired, and proceeded to Jamaica. The Coast Guard determined that the cause of the fire was a cargo light left on, which I don't believe. This heap of metal that I'm holding is the melted cargo light and all that's left of the *Port*. She was sold, renamed the *Poet*, and disappeared in the North Atlantic in 1980 with all hands, a couple of them friends of mine. The Coast Guard and the National Transportation Safety Board decided that a freak wave caused her to sink. I believe that her cargo of grain shifted and rolled her over. I've seen ships filled with grain up to the coamings of their huge hatches later develop a slight list at sea because the grain still had not settled.

Mr. Bullock:

The *MV Green Point* was leaving Singapore one night in 1998, on her maiden voyage for Central Gulf Lines, when a Greek tanker ran into her stern. No one was injured, and all of our damage was above the water line. We spent a week in a Singapore shipyard having the hole patched and then were off to Japan.

RESCUES

Commodore Alexanderson:

The Master of U.S. Lines' *SS America's* was Harry Manning, like myself a graduate of the New York Nautical School. He was known as "Rescue Harry" because he participated in so many rescues at sea. Manning, always a colorful man, wore a mink coat on the bridge. Like a few masters, he prohibited smoking on the bridge. Manning had been Amelia Earhart's navigator and was badly injured in a crash with her in Hawaii. During his one-year recuperation, she found another navigator. That man disappeared with her in the Pacific in the late-1930s.

Captain Schindler:

During the U.S. Naval blockade in the Cuban missile crisis of 1962, I was Third Mate on the tanker *SS Mission Buenaventura* bound for Venezuela. In the Mona Passage, between Cuba and Haiti, we picked up two Cubans escaping in a rowboat. Once aboard, they ate everything they could find, entered crew rooms, and threatened them. We locked the Cubans in the Shelter Deck. There they broke into the Bosun's and Steward's stores and got sick after eating a whole case of pineapple. We were glad to see them put ashore in Venezuela.

We again picked-up two fleeing Cubans in the Straits of Florida. Empty gasoline cans kept their small swamped boat afloat. We carried them to the U.S.

At the end of 1983, three days out of Pearl Harbor bound for Alaska, on the Third Mate's watch a boat crossed the *SS Hudson's* bow. I stopped the ship, took aboard a Canadian couple, and put their dismasted trimaran under tow. They had built the trimaran and sailed it around the world twice. At fifteen knots we towed it 1704 miles to Alaska in less than five days. The trimaran was repaired. The couple sailed back home to Vancouver and beached it. Their story appeared in *Sail* magazine. I still get Christmas cards from them.

Captain Smeenk:

Steaming in the Straits of Florida on a quiet night about 1993, the bow lookout on a Lykes ship heard a yell, reported it to the mate on watch, and the Captain turned the ship around. Using the searchlight we found two escaping Cubans on an inflatable raft. One was delirious from drinking seawater and had to be carried. The other walked up our accommodation ladder. We lost the raft with their papers. A U.S. Coast Guard helicopter took them off.

Captain Sulzer:

About 1981, when I was Second Mate on the *LNG Aries*, we picked-up two loads of Boat People escaping Vietnam and brought them to our discharge port in Japan. The Japanese would not take them. En route back to Sumatra, one of them delivered her first child with the help of the ship's officers. Her husband slept through the delivery. The mother named her Aries. Being born on a U.S. ship, she could claim U.S. citizenship. All the refugees were put ashore in Singapore.

Ms. Preston:

My only rescue occurred during my last year at sea, 1987. I was Chief Mate on the *SS Exxon Baltimore* on the twelve to four A.M. watch in the Caribbean Sea en route to Panama. Three Costa Rican fishermen in a sixteen-foot boat with twin Mercury outboard motors, ran out of gas after a compass malfunction. Our diesel fuel was of no use to them. The owner wanted his boat brought aboard, but we had no equipment to do it. Our crew translated by bullhorn. The owner left his boat, and we discharged them in Panama.

SEA STORIES

Captain Carter:

During the Great Depression, the steady job of Assistant Pier Superintendent seemed attractive. When I was Second Mate on Isthmian Lines' *SS Steel Trader*, I discussed the possibility with the Pier Superintendent in Honolulu. He told me that, if I would marry his wife's sister, I had the job. I went to dinner with the Pier Superintendent's family. After seeing the sister, I decided to stay at sea.

One night, en route to the Panama Canal, I was standing watch with an AB who had joined the ship in Honolulu. I knew the Morse code well and heard a request to relay to a ship ahead the description of a fugitive thought to be aboard her. As he steered the ship, the compass illuminated my AB. In my opinion, he resembled the description of the fugitive, and I had the Radio Officer and Captain confirm it. We sent a message that he was aboard. U.S. Marshals met him in Balboa.

Commodore Alexanderson:

When I reported to U.S. Lines' *SS America* as Executive Officer in 1946, I expected a briefing on my duties. However, the only advice from my predecessor, and probably the reason for his departure, was, "Don't proposition a girl on the dance floor. It echoes all over the room."

While commanding the Troop Ship *John Ericson* during World War II, United States Lines' Commodore John W. Anderson, a very kind man, picked up a cocker spaniel and named him Chota Peg, Hindustani for a small drink. His wife did not like the dog, so Anderson could not take him home. While Anderson was on vacation from the *SS United States*, Chota Peg died. I buried him at sea, made an entry in the ship's logbook, and sent a cable to Anderson. The dog's obituary appeared in *The New York Times*.

Captain Atkinson:

Right after World War II, I was Master of the Liberty Ship *William Grayson* in commercial service. After we discharged coal, locomotives and timber at Cherbourg, France an AB remained behind. He was arrested by French Customs for bringing ashore ninety-nine pairs of nylon stockings and 50,000 lighter flints.

At the end of 1947, I did a favor for Isbrandtsen's Port Captain, Kurt Carlsen, who later became famous for staying with his sinking *SS Flying Enterprise* in the North Atlantic. I went as Chief Mate on a little, World War II laker bound for the Bay of Fundy in Nova Scotia for lay-up. The ship was tied up at a dock. The Bay of Fundy is known for its range of tide. When the tide went out, she was on timbers on the bottom. The water in the bay was at least a half-mile away, and people were driving cars on the sand.

Captain Fowler:

In early 1948, I became Master of the Liberty Ship *Thomas R. Marshall* and made several voyages to Italy with coal. Because there was never time for an adequate search before departure, several times stowaways came aboard. In Naples, three of them hid in the shaft alley and came up on deck after departure. I put them ashore in Gibraltar for repatriation.

My Third Mate was friendly with two Italians who had been deported from San Francisco and lived in Genoa. All of them were entrepreneurs. At sailing time, there were two Italians on the dock yelling for money. I learned that the Third Mate had taken $1,000 to allow them to stow away in the officers' shower room. He told the Chief Mate that they were there, and the Mate put them off the ship.

On the next trip, we went to Sivona, west of Genoa. The Third Mate had received a letter from one of the stowaways threatening his life. He didn't leave the ship or even walk on the shore side of it.

On the same voyage, an Ordinary Seaman came back drunk before sailing and became obstreperous. The Chief Mate handcuffed him to his bunk. When we sailed at 9 pm, I heard a commotion on the foredeck. The Ordinary had to be on bow lookout and was trying to drag his bunk up there with him.

In 1949 I was given command of the *SS American Starling*, a Liberty Ship carrying Army cargo. During the voyage I developed a toothache. There was no dentist in the Azores, so I had to wait until our next discharge port, Casablanca, Morocco. The agent took me to a dentist, who injected my jaw from a syringe big enough for a horse and pulled my tooth. By the time we sailed for Galveston the next day, my jaw had frozen. For ten days, until my jaw loosened, I lived on soup through a straw stuck in the corner of my mouth.

On a voyage from LaSpezia, Italy to Paramaribo, Dutch Guyana a Messman stabbed another Messman during an argument. The Mate tended to the injured man's wounds in the ship's hospital. The assailant was quite worried and told me that he had thrown his knife overboard. I logged him, that is, made the incident a matter of record in the ship's official log. The injured Messman recovered and continued the voyage. At pay-off in Gulfport, Mississippi I told the U.S. Shipping Commissioner that I wanted the assailant charged. The Commissioner was in a hurry to get home to New Orleans and talked me out of it.

When I was Master of the *SS American Starling*, a stowaway from LaGuira, Venezuela was found just prior to arrival in Aruba. I had him locked up while the ship was in Aruba. On arrival in Maricaibo, I reported him to the boarding officials, expecting them to take him ashore. They wouldn't take him because he claimed to be a Costa Rican. I also tried to land him at various Caribbean islands, including the U.S. Virgin Islands, without success. The Chief Mate had the stowaway working on deck with the Bosun. Then he refused to work, claiming not to understand English. The Mate locked him in the forepeak hatch after dinner. That night a storm hit, and we took water over the bow. When the Mate went to feed him breakfast, he found a scared stowaway praying in English. After three days in New York, the Costa Rican Consul finally got him off the ship for return to Costa Rica.

I put a Spanish stowaway from LaPolice, France off the *SS American Oriole* by lifeboat in the Atlantic Ocean onto the eastbound *SS American Robin*. I had led her Master to believe that the stowaway was a female I could not keep aboard.

Captain White:

In 1936, I was an Ordinary Seaman on the yacht *Happy Days*, *in* Havana, Cuba to load rum and cigars for the owner and his guests. I was walking with a Messman, who later became a Captain, on the main street when six of our fellow crewmen invited us into a Lincoln touring car. We got in, saw the driver of the car pinned low in the back seat, and realized that they were drunk. The driver wriggled loose, jumped out of the car, and called the police. After a scuffle, they took all of us to jail. Fortunately, the driver said that the Messman and I were not involved, so we were released.

The crew sent a request to the Captain to bail them out. While waiting, they pooled their money and bailed themselves out. The Captain was awakened, came in from the anchorage, and then had to find his crew in a bar. We were all in the doghouse for several days.

Captain McCarthy:

"Fiddlin' Schultz" was a very capable Mormac Master with one failing - he played the violin. When he sailed as

Third, Second, and Chief Mate, there was a mute on his violin, but when he became Master, the mute came off. As Second Mate with him on the Liberty Ship *Sherwood Anderson* in 1944, I had the twelve to four watch. Schultz liked to practice scales early in the morning. They reminded me of my aunt, a professional violinist. My protests that I couldn't sleep didn't stop Schultz.

Mr. Ramsey:

The *SS Flying Gull* carried twelve passengers in Isbrandtsen's around-the world service. One of them was a very nice high school teacher from Connecticut. She was interested in everything about the *Gull*, the sea, and the weather. One day at lunch, she asked the other Third Mate, the author, a question about the lights of the aurora borealis. He loaned her his meteorology textbook. By dinner, she had read the book and commented to me on the amount of knowledge necessary to become a Mate. The *Gull's* Chief Mate, Henry Lexius, liked to brag that he had not stood a watch in twenty years. He spent his days in his office playing loud, martial music on his tape recorder. The schoolteacher, of course, had heard the music. I told her that being a Mate took more than playing the tape recorder loudly.

Captain Schindler:

After going from Seattle to Bombay with grain on the *SS Henry* in the late-1960s, we made an unscheduled stop in Kuwait for a return load of oil. The result was an around-the-world trip. We ran out of toilet paper and food, except for liver, hot dogs, and apricots. The Cook did everything possible with liver, hot dogs, and apricots for two weeks, but I will never eat any of them again. In Bizerte, Tunisia we took on toilet paper, one side like waxed paper and the other like sandpaper. I was never sure which side to use.

On the same ship we arrived Port Arthur, Texas from Bombay, when a drunken, obnoxious, U.S. Customs informant came aboard asking to buy drugs. As crewmembers escorted him down the gangway, he began firing a pistol. Otis, a well-liked young Wiper, grabbed the informant around the shoulders and was shot in the chest. As usual, the dock phone was busy. The Second Mate used the radio in a passing taxi to call for an ambulance. The big Bosun beat the assailant with his own gun, knocking out his teeth, and complaining that the weapon was too light to hurt him. The crew handcuffed the informant to the rail and wanted to hang him right there. The Port Arthur Police arrived, said it was the Sheriff's problem and left. Otis survived.

All Egyptian Pilots are cowboys. One was approaching the dock in Alexandria too fast, so ordered the starboard anchor dropped. When told that it wasn't holding, he ordered the port anchor dropped. The Chief Mate dropped the port anchor, but it landed on the dock. You should have seen those Arabs run.

I ran coastwise with black oil on the *Kent*, sister ship to the *Henry*, and then with grain to Bombay, where the ship was sold to foreigners. I flew home via Delhi and Moscow, and sent a cable to my wife, "On my way home. From Russia with love."

One night in Gaeta, Italy in the early 1980s, when I was Master of the *SS Hudson*, the Chief Mate called me to the Pump Room. An AB named Red was lying on his back with a twenty-foot long trail of blood coming from his right ear. The Mate claimed that Red had fallen. Red died in a hospital the next day. The Chief Mate, who was also the leader of a motorcycle gang, was later arrested in the U.S. for beating someone. In prison he bragged that he had killed an AB. I believe that he killed Red and sent this information to the FBI.

Captain Smeenk:

After the unexpected scrapping of the *SS Steel Worker* in Taiwan 1971, we all had a lot of luggage. I had been on the ship for three years and had new, large stereo speakers. Some of the crew had been aboard for twenty years. The Captain and his wife had their golf clubs. He insisted that Isthmian ship our personal effects back to the U.S. on the same plane with us. We all had to spend two nights in a Kaoshiung hotel. On check-in, all the local whores greeted us. The next morning in the hotel lobby, the Captain, a very pleasant man, gave the crew a draw against wages. He said, "I never thought I'd be giving out a draw in a whore house." The girls discretely stayed away while the Captain was giving out the money.

Ms. Preston:

On the *SS Exxon Washington* I met my husband, Bill, a mate who graduated from the State University of New York Maritime College. We married in 1980, but never again sailed together due to Exxon's policy that spouses had to sail on different ships. I call *Exxon Washington* a "love boat" because I know of three couples who sailed on her and later married. My husband stayed with Exxon a year longer than I did and then quit for a Master's job on a 27,000-ton, semi-submersible, oil drilling rig in the North Sea.

The older crewmen had already seen many changes in their seagoing lives and were much more accepting of me, as a woman, than I anticipated. They expected nothing of a woman in the first place. When I performed my job well, it was considered better than they ever dreamed possible. I had a whole lot easier time with my peers after getting married because then no one bothered me.

By 1981, I was sailing Second Mate on the *SS Exxon Florence.* I did not tell the company that I was pregnant for fear they would make me leave the ship with only six months' maternity leave. Cleaning tanks in Louisiana in August, the Captain commented that I was slower than usual. I finally told the Chief Mate that I was suffering from morning sickness.

Sailing during my second pregnancy was a lot tougher because of the sixteen to twenty-hour days of the Chief Mate on a three-Mate ship. My second daughter was born in February 1988, and I got my Master's license five weeks later.

Mr. Bullock:

As Third Mate on the *SS OMI Missouri* in 1989, I saw pirates in powerful tugs and fishing boats along the coast of Malaysia at night. We turned on all the deck lights and patrolled the deck with fire hoses, but did not have to repel any boarders.

The closest I came to combat was on the tanker *SS Gus W. Darnell*, anchored for two weeks in the Persian Gulf in 1991. Six Philippino crewmen got drunk and went after the Americans in the crew with fire axes. The Captain and I broke up the riot with no injuries.

PASSING TIME

Captain Carter:

While sailing, I took up photography and developed my own prints.

Commodore Alexanderson:

I enjoyed the quiet time on the container ship *SS American Legion* after having the responsibility of entertaining in the passenger ships. Passengers expected to meet me unless there was bad weather, when I was on the bridge. Some passengers were difficult and thought that the ship was their private yacht.

United States Lines expected the Commodore to make Christmas trips as an example for the crew, so I was away from home nine Christmases in a row. It was also company policy that family members could not travel on the ships with us.

Captain Dick Patterson left the *SS America* because he wanted time to paint and write.

Rear Admiral Richard Oakes Patterson, USNR (Retired), a 1923 graduate of the New York Nautical School, retired from United States Lines in 1970. He won several prizes for his marine paintings, exhibited on ships he commanded.

Captain Fowler:

As far as hobbies, I once tried taking and developing photographs after I saw an advertisement in a magazine. I still have the photos.

Mr. Ramsey:

With the crew down to twenty one people and each of them doing about two and a half jobs on what I call these "twenty-mule team ships," there is not a lot of spare time. Yet, thirty days at sea during a ninety-day voyage brings about burnout. I bring a sea bag full of books for a trip and spend a lot of time reading.

I've organized fly-catching contests. In Chittagong, Bangladesh flies were plentiful. The Chief Cook won with over 500 flies. The Third Mate was runner-up with 310. Prizes, in the form of sweatshirts or caps, came from the slop chest. Once, the Captain went on vacation without awarding the prizes, and the flies were mailed to his home in Italy.

I've organized cribbage tournaments with a $10.00-entry fee and 50% of the gross receipts to the ship's video fund.

On the LNG ships the average age of the crew was about twenty-two, so physical activity was preferred. The body-builders had a gym. There was basketball in the bow, water polo in the swimming pool, and volleyball, all arranged by the Recreation Officer designated by the Captain.

For years, I've maintained a blackboard on the bridge featuring cryptograms, historically significant dates, unusual abbreviations, mysteries and thoughts for the days.

Captain Schindler:

I felt that I really earned my money as Master on tankers. The only free time I got was on a long voyage, say, twenty days from the Panama Canal to Subic Bay in the Philippines in ballast. I always brought books of interest to me at the time, for example, paleoanthropology or the history section of my set of Great Books of the

Western World, and read them like a homework assignment.

I spent three of my six years on the tanker *SS Henry* building a four-foot long model of her.

Captain Smeenk:

I used to read a lot of history at sea, but as Chief Mate I worked twelve-plus hours a day, eight on the bridge as a watch-stander navigating and reacting to situations that arise, and four more doing cargo paperwork.

There is not the diversity of cargoes of a few years ago. Now the boom ships carry mostly bagged goods, and the loading and stowage is supervised by ship management companies, although the Chief Mate is responsible. Schools in India and the Philippines train ship managers. When sailing as Master, I was always on call for emergencies or navigation and do the paperwork associated with the crew and entering and clearing ports. On trips with many ports close together this can be hectic.

Captain Sulzer:

At sea I read, studied, completed Navy correspondence courses, or collected artifacts and explored in ports.

Ms. Preston:

When I first went with Exxon, there was more camaraderie among the crews, no movies, rather cards and stories of World War II in the lounge. Now they have compact discs and walk man radios for individual entertainment. Crews are so small and fatigued from making ports every three - five days, that they can only work, eat and sleep.

I think that the Captains and Chief Mates can set the tone for congeniality. For example, I told the Third Mate that she was responsible for providing a fresh Christmas tree on the *SS Exxon Baltimore*. She brought aboard not one, but three trees and presents and stockings for all the crew. At midnight on another Christmas on the same ship, the Captain was on the bridge for stormy weather. So that no one would miss the Christmas spirit, he read the Christmas passage from the Bible by the light of the radar.

ON THE BEACH

A seafarer between deep-sea jobs is "on the beach."

Captain Carter:

While on strike in 1936, in San Pedro, California I got my Master's license and renewed it ten times, last in 1984.

Captain Fowler:

On March 11, 1952, I wrote American Foreign Steamship Company requesting a relief as Master. I intended to become a Docking Pilot for the Baker Whitely Towing Company in Baltimore, but I couldn't get into the tugboat union.

I went as AB on the *Esso Delivery Number 7* carrying 5,000 barrels of heating oil, gasoline, and kerosene on the Chesapeake Bay, then got a Pilot's license for the bay and was made a Mate. After twenty days of six hours on and six off, we got ten days off. We loaded at the Esso docks in Baltimore for eastern bay ports like Easton, Salisbury, and Crisfield, Maryland and Onancock, Virginia. At Norfolk we loaded for ports on the western side of the bay, West Point, Tappahannock, and Fredericksburg, Virginia and Leonardtown, Maryland.

After a year with Esso, to have more time at home, I became a Mate on a fireboat in Baltimore Harbor. At the Fire Department School it was difficult to keep up with recruits half my age. Though when it came to tying knots, I was able to help my classmates

I worked four days from 7 A.M. to 5 P.M., had a day off, then four days from 5 P.M. to 7 A.M. and had a day off. Some days there was nothing to do but shine bright work, but, when the alarm sounded, it was an organized madhouse. Once, a freight car on my own pier, Pier 3 in Canton, caught fire, and at the same time, my Chief

Engineer had a fatal heart attack. My boat was a very large steamboat and could throw a lot of water from its pipes. I became good at handling it, but didn't care for the military aspect of the Fire Department. After two years on the fireboat, I decided to go back to sea.

Captain White:

By age thirty five, I had been master of eleven different ships - tankers, dry cargo, ro-ro, yachts, tugs, and salvage vessels. I accepted a two-year contract as a Pilot in the Panama Canal.

We lived near Cristobal, so most of my assignments were on vessels southbound from Colon to Balboa. Pilots made four transits a week on a variety of vessels, from U.S. Navy ships to foreign motor vessels. Each vessel was new as far as crews and nationalities. About ninety percent were foreign flag. I had never before been on a foreign flag ship. For someone like myself, who enjoys meeting people, the job was very interesting. On the United Fruit Company ships I met some of the men I had sailed with during World War II.

Every vessel transiting the Canal must have a Pilot. I took the little yacht *Wanderer III* from the Cristobal Yacht Club to the Balboa Yacht Club in eighteen hours, taking the tiller myself, rather than giving steering orders. The owners were Sue and Eric Hisock. He had been a tailor of men's clothes, and she did textile work. When Eric's eyesight went bad, they sold their little home on England's Isle of Wight and purchased a sailing vessel. They covered European waters and were in the process of a trip around the world. To defray their costs Eric wrote books about yachting, and they became prominent in yachting circles. A picture of me appears in his book *Around the World in Wanderer III*.

I did not usually take northbound ships, but one day the dispatcher sent me to Balboa for any of three arriving ships. I was piloting the Greek flag *Christos M* in

Miraflores Lock and noticed the bunk in the corner of the wheelhouse. There I was again on my first command, the Liberty Ship *Frank Adair Monroe*.

Halfway through the Canal ships cross Gatun Lake and enter a seven-mile long cut through the solid rock of the Continental Divide. If a Pilot had a sluggish or bad-handling ship, he asked the dispatcher for "a clear cut," so that he would not meet any other ship. Once, a northbound Pilot, who stuttered, asked for and received a clear cut. A southbound Pilot immediately informed the dispatcher that he was on a bad-handling ship around a bend in the cut, and the ships would pass in a few minutes. The stuttering northbound Pilot asked him to give him all the room he could. The southbound Pilot replied, "I have a bad-handling ship, too. You can have half of the cut."

The highlight of my work as a Pilot was being on the team of five Pilots assigned to navigate the aircraft carrier *USS Tulagi* through the Canal. She was 950 feet long and 109 feet wide. The locks are 1000 feet long and 110 feet wide, so there were only inches on each side to play with. The shoreside engines, called mules, disappeared under the flight deck when pulling the *Tulagi* into a lock. There was a Pilot at each corner of the flight deck. I was the one on the port quarter. The Senior Pilot was on the bridge. When my corner of the ship was about to brush the lock's wall, I would say, "Starboard quarter, brake." The mule operator would brake on his wire, pulling the vessel back a little from the wall. Nonetheless, loud scraping sounds went through the ship.

The pay and time off were good. The heat, humidity, and 160 to 180 inches annual rainfall were particularly hard on families used to a temperate climate. My son liked living in the Canal Zone, but my wife and daughter did not. At the end of my contract, we moved back to California, and I went back to sea with Isthmian Line.

153

Mr. Ramsey:

When Farrell Lines took over American Export Lines in 1978, the company was looking for someone with Chief Mate's experience to be the liaison with the ship's officers, the agents, and the stevedores in the Orient. I took the job, based in Tokyo, because I liked both the Orient and the challenge. I worked with American Export Lines' agent, Harry Hamilton, Port Captain Don Lippert, the U.S. military, shippers, and, of course, the Japanese. To assist the Chief Mate, I rode each ship to Korea. When the regular office personnel went on vacation, I worked in Hong Kong, where I met my wife.

Three years later, the company was closing its service to the Far East, and I needed sea time to renew my license. I went on the SS *Exmouth*, a small Victory ship, and on the SS *Flying Spray*, a C-1. My brother was Second Assistant Engineer on both ships with me. We thought the assignments were a publicity stunt by the company.

Closure of the Suez Canal ended around-the-world liner service, and containerization was increasing, reducing the need for American Export Lines' boom ships. Farrell's takeover of AEL forced a confrontation between Farrell's deck officers' union, the MM&P, and AEL's company union, the Brotherhood of Marine Officers (BMO). AEL's deck officers lost out. After seventeen years with AEL, I found myself unemployed. We were given the choice of going with the MM&P or the Marine Engineers Beneficial Association (MEBA) District 1, which had absorbed the BMO about 1980. I chose MEBA, a good decision because I'm now eligible to retire.

While unemployed, I went with the U.S. Army Corps of Engineers on a big dredge, the *Harding*, as Third Mate, Second Mate and then Chief Mate. In winter, we dredged San Francisco Bay and in summer, fishing and lumber ports on the coast of Oregon and in the Columbia River. Thanks to twin screws and bow thrusters, we got in and out of unique places. I met some very talented ship handlers and got good experience.

I went back to deep-sea when the opportunity came. Between ships, at home in California, I pursue real estate interests, sail boats, garden, take long walks with my dog, and make car trips.

Captain Schindler:

Vacations were three months after a year of sailing when I started going to sea in 1962 and progressed to four months on and four months off at the end of my career. This schedule gave me half of every summer and every other Christmas at home. It was a nice life, breaking $100,000 a year and touring the U.S. in our motor home.

I also worked as a Port Captain on my vacations, supervising tank cleaning and crew changes, for example, escorting forty Indians from New York to a foreign flag ship in Texas.

Captain Glen:

It was difficult to get vacations when American Export Lines was operating fifty two cargo ships, three passenger ships and the Nuclear Ship *Savannah* during the Vietnam War. Due to the training needed on the *Savannah*, we could only rotate vacations among ourselves. I built-up nine months' vacation, so I bought a motor home and with a girlfriend and a dog toured the U.S. and Canada for a number of months.

When I return to a ship from vacation, I'm never sure if I'm back in the groove or back in a rut.

Captain Smeenk:

In 1973, I had accumulated considerable vacation time and began taking specialized courses at MM&P's Maritime

Institute of Graduate Studies (MITAGS,) outside Baltimore, prior to taking my Master's license examination.

I spent nine months traveling on my own in Taiwan, Thailand, Burma, and by train down the East Coast of the Malay Peninsula to Singapore.

During four months as Chief Mate and Master of a 130-foot oil rig supply boat in Indonesia, I mastered ship handling.

In 1975, I became a part-time instructor at MITAGS in the use of radar in collision avoidance and have continued there on and off.

As a bachelor I enjoyed going to sea. I married at thirty eight and spent six months at sea for many years. Now I ship out of the MM&P Hall and have plenty of time between trips for my house in Washington, DC, museums, concerts, and travel with my wife in the U.S. and overseas.

Captain Wanner:

In my spare time I do a lot of hunting and fishing. I'm outdoors most of the time.

Captain Sulzer:

Until May 1980, I was teaching navigation and working on my Master's Degree in Transportation Management at Fort Schuyler, so I missed most of the MM&P and BMO tumult.

Starting in 1988, for a few years, I was Vice President for Operations of Sea Line Company, developing hydroplane passenger ferries for use in New York City. The company was bought by an Australian company and still operates.

My preference is engineering, and I do it in my shoreside business. I have a Panamanian Second Assistant Engineer's license and a U.S. Coast Guard license as Third Assistant Engineer. I was going to switch jobs on an LNG ship with a Third Assistant Engineer who also had a Third Mate's license, but in September, 1996, I came ashore as Director of Industrial Relations for Keystone Shipping Company, operator of thirty tankers out of Philadelphia.

I spent a year in 1995-1996, doing curriculum development at the MEBA Engineering School in Easton, Maryland.

On my vacations from the sea, I worked as a marine consultant, operated my father's fleet of barges in Philadelphia, and restored our 1816 farmhouse south of Philadelphia. When I got off a ship in Japan, my wife joined me for sightseeing. I like variety. I'd drive a truck if I wanted to stay on the same run.

Ms. Preston:

After my first daughter was born in 1982, I stayed ashore for fourteen months as an agent in Exxon's Baytown, Texas office. My father hoped that I would be the first female Master in the U.S. Merchant Marine and took care of my daughter, while I returned to sea.

My second daughter was born in February 1988, and I got my Master's license five weeks later. I wanted to sail as Master, but advancement at Exxon was slow. My parents raised my first daughter at their home in Pensacola, Florida. I didn't want them to have to do it again and miss her childhood, too. I quit my job with Exxon. My father calls my oldest daughter "the $10,000-baby" because the wife of a Kings Point alumnus had offered $10,000 each to the first alumna sailing as Master and Chief Engineer.

I would like to have seen more foreign ports, but it wasn't a possibility due to the few remaining boom ships and short port stays. I made only one foreign trip with Exxon, to a shipyard in Korea as Second Mate on the *SS Exxon Boston*.

From 1989 to 1994, I worked at the Federal Maritime Administration in Washington, DC in the Maintenance and

Repair Section for the Ready Reserve Force of laid-up ships. I did the writing that I always wanted to do, technical manuals and marine product evaluations.

I got a Master's degree in Public Administration from the University of West Florida in 1994. From August 1994 until October 1997, I headed an environmental program at the Naval Aviation Depot, Pensacola, Florida.

In 1998, I became the Safety Officer at Alabama Shipyard in Mobile, Alabama. My husband was ashore as a manager with the National Response Corporation, handling oil spills. He has returned to sea as Master of an oil drilling ship in the Gulf of Mexico, working three weeks on and three weeks off. We have one daughter in boarding school and one still at home. I really miss going to sea for a living and would like to go back someday.

Mr. Bullock:

About a year after I came back from Operation Desert Storm on the *USNS Capella*, I came down with an unexplained, constant, one hundred- degree fever and had to quit sailing. I think that the combination of chemical biological warfare, smoke from oil well fires, and fumes from JP5 and JP8 high-test jet fuels made me sick. My wife and I moved to the clean air of Maine, and my health improved. I worked at carpentry, landscaping, and installing pumps for wells.

I spent the spring and summer of 1996 as Mate on Maine Maritime Academy's research vessel *MV Argo Marine*, 200 tons and eighty feet long. Under contract to the U.S. Army Corps of Engineers, we took water samples and core samples of the ocean bottom off the coast of New England and went as far south as New Jersey.

My wife likes me home at least six months a year. When I'm not shipping with MM&P, I do some land surveying. It's great to be out in the Maine woods. I also do a little repair and body work on cars.

EBBING

A tidal current moving away from land Is ebbing.

Captain Carter:

There were no unions when I started with Isthmian in 1929. Captains and Chief Engineers got one or two weeks' vacation and could take their wives on coastwise trips. If they took vacations, they missed their ships and had to wait without pay for another ship. No one else in the crew received paid vacations.

By 1936, I was a member of the MM&P. The maritime unions called a strike against all U.S. ships for higher wages. I was in San Pedro as Second Mate on the *SS Steel Trader*, got an apartment in Long Beach, and was a Picket Captain there. As a result of the strike, wages for Chief Mate went up to about $185 per month, Second Mate to $150, and Third Mate to $135. I calculated that it would take me seven years to recoup the wages I lost during the strike.

Commodore Alexanderson:

Large airplanes were taking U.S. Lines' transatlantic passengers, so the *SS United States* began cruising in the Caribbean in 1961. Once, we added a thirty-nine-day cruise to Curacao, Netherland Antilles; Rio de Janiero, Capetown and Port Elizabeth, South Africa; Luanda, Angola; the Canary Islands, and Madeira.

The *United States* arrived in New York on November 8, 1969, after Walter Kiddee purchased United States Lines, and then proceeded to Newport News, Virginia for her annual dry docking and Coast Guard inspection. Preparations were underway for a trip around the world via the Panama Canal. I was at home in Garden City, New York, when the Marine Superintendent called to tell me that the *United States* was being laid-up. He instructed me to return to the ship and pay-off the crew by Thanksgiving.

Crewmembers transferred our foodstuffs to a U.S. Lines Mariner class ship in the yard in Norfolk, for transport back to New York. The Chief Engineer and I stayed on the dead ship until April, 1970, when she was shifted by five tugs to Norfolk International Terminal. In 1973, the Federal Maritime Administration preserved the ship by sealing it and placing aboard 13 dehumidifiers. Richard H. Hadley, of United States Cruises, bought the ship from the U.S. Government for $5,000,000 in 1979, with plans to put her back in the cruise business.

The *United States* remained at a pier in Norfolk until she was sold for $2,600,000 in 1992. She was towed to turkey and then to Philadelphia in 1996.

The November 25, 1986 edition of the *New York Times* reported that United States Lines filed a petition for bankruptcy on November 24, 1986, suspending worldwide shipping services.

Captain Atkinson:

Unfortunately, despite the billions spent for national defense, our shortsighted politicians have undermined the state maritime academies by cutting out funds for their operations, training ships, and cruises and have allowed our merchant fleet to dwindle almost to the point of non-existence.

Three times during my own career at sea, the old-timers have been rounded up and put aboard ships because of a shortage of experienced officers and seamen. It could happen again. I, for one, have kept my Master's license active in case of need. We are bound to run out of old-timers eventually, if no new men come into the industry, or if there is no industry for them to come into.

Captain White:

The demands of maritime unions in 1936 were justified. Food was just edible, and we had pads instead of mattresses. A big intercoastal company like Luckenbach paid ABs $35.00 per month, while we read of Edgar F. Luckenbach spending big money on his wives and girlfriends. In later years, unions became a detriment. I've heard it said that we're the highest paid, most unemployed seafaring people in the world. We priced ourselves out of the market and sounded the death knell for the American Merchant Marine.

Admiral Bauman:

Isbrandtsen Steamship Company bought Pocahontas Fuel Company in 1953. I worked my way up to Chief Mate, but never became Master because the coal boats were being sold as oil replaced coal as a fuel. I went with United Fruit Company as Third Mate for a few trips from New York to Baltimore to Havana, Cuba with general cargo and then to some banana port for loading. Leaving Havana in 1957, a cable from my wife said I'd been accepted into the U.S. Coast Guard as a Lieutenant.

In 1968, I commanded a Coast Guard Division in Da Nang, Vietnam. I received a letter from the Military Sea Transportation Service telling me that they had openings for licensed officers. This was in reply to my application to MSTS, twenty years earlier.

Mr. Ramsey:

During my years at sea, I've seen a decrease in vessel traffic because there are fewer ships afloat. I completed a trip from Chittagong, Bangladesh to New Orleans via the Cape of Good Hope, two thirds of the way around the world, and saw visually or on radar under ten ships.

To say the least, the U.S. Merchant Marine is a depressed industry. Big companies, like Farrell and U.S. Lines, are gone. The Third World is gaining in construction and crewing of ships. There are too many officers for the available jobs on U.S. ships, so they have to find other types of jobs. Also, many U.S. companies are non-union, making for low wages and fewer benefits.

Captain Schindler:

The biggest changes I saw while going to sea concerned automation. Firemen and Wipers were replaced by the position Qualified Member Engine Department (QMED). Each ship has three QMEDs as day-workers for maintenance and repairs, leaving only one engineer on watch at all times. I observed this effective, cost-saving operation for three years. Then the U.S. Coast Guard decided that no "procedure" was posted for QMEDs and ordered them returned to Engine Room watches, meaning that the QMEDs sat in the Control Room reading books. The maintenance and repairs they had been doing were accomplished by paying them overtime. It took a year to settle this dispute, an example of the U.S. Coast Guard working against the interests of the U.S. Merchant Marine.

Crew sizes have been cut below safe limits, from forty-two to under twenty-five people. Automatic cargo systems on tankers made crew reduction possible. One person in a Control Room could open and close valves with a switch. However, as the valves got old, the switches did not work, so we went back to operating hand wheels, but with fewer crewmembers to do it.

In the Steward's Department reductions have meant unappetizing "TV dinners" served cafeteria style, down from the seven entrees on the Keystone ships I sailed on.

The attitudes of crews and owners make up the biggest problem for the U.S. Merchant Marine. On foreign ships the owners provide meals in a dining salon like a hotel, parquet floors, and a carpeted recreation room with video cassettes. The result is crew pride in their community, the ship. American owners provide none of these amenities, witness my six-foot long room on the *SS Solomon B. Turman* with its six-foot bunk, a little, fold-down desk, one chair, and an imitation leather sofa. Transient U.S. union crews are only interested in how much overtime they can earn. The maritime unions foster members' loyalty to the union, not the ships they serve.

Captain Glen:

I was Second Mate on American Export Lines' *SS Flying Cloud*, a C-2 we took to a ship breaker's yard in Taiwan for scrapping in 1972.

In 1978, American Export Lines was folding and was bought by Farrell Lines. In the beginning of 1979, when I was Chief Mate on the *SS Export Ambassador*, we were given an ultimatum that, if we wanted to keep our jobs, we had to join the MM&P and stay with Farrell Lines. I wasn't happy with this prospect and left after fourteen years with the Brotherhood of Marine Officers and American Export Lines.

Captain Smeenk:

After obtaining my Second Mate's license, in 1969 I began sailing for Isthmian Lines, a wholly owned subsidiary of States Marine Lines. Over a four-year period, coinciding with massive U.S. Agency for International Development (AID) shipments, we carried food to India. Return cargoes from Chittagong and Chalna, Bangladesh consisted of Hessian cloth for carpet backing, in rolls twelve to fourteen feet long and three feet in diameter, tea, cashew nuts, and Indian-manufactured clothes. Isthmian's liner service was ending because their ships, like my *SS Steel Worker* and *Steel Maker*, were over twenty years old. Using worldwide averages, insurers and shipper wouldn't bother with ships over twenty five years old because of the likelihood or accidents or breakdowns. Some countries, for example, Indonesia and Egypt, legislated against old ships using their ports for safety reasons.

In the absence of return cargoes, Isthmian relied on military cargoes to Vietnam and AID shipments of wheat and foodstuffs to India. U.S. law dictates that a percentage of AID cargoes moves in U.S. ships. Outbound, old U.S. ships carried AID cargoes, which the consignees had to accept, but returned empty because shippers wouldn't use them.

After discharge in India in 1971, we were shocked when the *SS Steel Worker* was ordered to a Taiwan scrap yard. She was a twenty six-year-old C-3 cargo ship, but in good condition after recent repairs in Singapore.

At "Full Astern" we ran the ship onto a bank, until the screw wouldn't turn any more, put out two lines astern, and shut down the power plant. Ships next to us were being cut with torches into ten-foot square chunks, starting on the superstructure and proceeding down to the waterline. They rose in the water, as they became lighter. When only the double bottoms remained, a tractor pulled it onto the beach for final cuts. Later, the Taiwanese learned the value of accessories, like clocks and wooden steering wheels, and made certain that the U.S. crews did not remove them. Scrap yards in Taiwan closed because the space was needed for containerized cargoes. Scrapping is now done in the People's Republic of China, Thailand, and India.

I became Chief Mate on an old C-3 as Isthmian was selling off their ships. After ten months aboard, I signed on for one more trip to get the required twelve months' sea time as Chief Mate to sit for my Master's license. The trip turned out to be six and a half months long. We loaded general cargo and AID cargo at U.S. East Coast and Gulf ports for India. With no return cargo, we continued to Vietnam and loaded damaged military vehicles for repair in Taiwan.

About 1972, after discharging wheat in India, we proceeded to Taiwan, where we loaded AID fertilizer for Surabaja, Indonesia. To cross the bar at the entrance to Surabaja, just before high water, the ship proceeds at "Full Ahead" and stops the engine as she hits the bar to avoid damage to the propeller. Momentum propels the ship through the soft mud in a few minutes.

As Chief Mate, responsible for cargo, I had to have the ship cleaned. The charterer had allowed only $250.00 for rough cleaning. Consequently, by the time the ship returned to Houston, Texas, wheat had sprouted in the fertilizer residue in the holds and had to be cleaned out at the U.S. labor rate of $250.00 per hour.

We began a shuttle run from either Keelung or Kaohsiung, Taiwan to Surabaja, Indonesia with AID cargoes of fertilizer.

Lykes ran about ten boom ships and scrapped all of them between 1993 and 1995. In the fall of 1995, Lykes filed for Chapter Eleven bankruptcy protection. They continued running three old ships chartered from American President Lines (APL). Lykes also took back four large containerships they built overseas in the 1980s, but couldn't afford to operate when completed, and had chartered to APL.

I was Chief Mate on the *SS Charlotte Lykes* when she was scrapped in the summer of 1995. On a new moon, spring high tide we anchored in an estuary at Alang, about 120 miles north of Bombay. The *SS Margaret Lykes* had arrived a week earlier for scrapping. For liability reasons, an Indian crew took over and ran the *Charlotte Lykes*, at "Full Ahead," onto a mud bank. Beforehand, foreign crews climb down a Jacob's ladder into a lifeboat, row to the beach, and wade ashore. A tug meets American crews at the ship's gangway for a four-hour ride upstream to Bhavnaghar to clear Customs. Four hours on a bus brings the crew to a regional airport for a flight to Bombay or Delhi. *Charlotte's* crew flew to Bombay. The *Sheldon*

Lykes and *Adabelle Lykes* ran until the spring of 1996, when they were scrapped.

I lost my job with Lykes in the summer of 1995, took lots of paid vacation, collected unemployment, and worked on my house. Luckily, I was able to wait because, after I registered with the MM&P Hall in Baltimore, it was just short of a year until I got a job. I shipped as Second Mate on the *SS Nuevo San Juan*. She was one of five old U.S. Lines' containerships of the Lancer class built in 1979, 19,445 gross tons, about 720 feet long, ninety feet wide, with the house midships. They shuttled between Port Elizabeth, New Jersey; San Juan, Puerto Rico; Jacksonville, Florida; San Juan, and Port Elizabeth in fourteen days with twelve hours in each port.

MM&P Second and Third Mates no longer have permanent jobs and are dispatched to ships for four-month periods. Between thirty and ninety days they can take up to thirty days off. At the end of 120 days, they get off, reregister at an MM&P Hall, and wait for up to a year to bid on jobs. The bidding is based on the oldest card, or who's been waiting the longest. If a ship is out of the U.S. at the end of 120 days, a mate can stay with it until it returns to the U.S.

I had to wait until the end of 1998 to get another job, Second Mate on Sealand's *SS Galveston Bay*, a former U.S. Lines' container ship. We ran from U.S. East Coast ports to northern Europe, twenty-eight-day round trips with one day built-in for bad weather.

It took ten months and going cross-country to the MM&P Hall in Los Angeles to get another job, Third Mate on the *SS Sealand Defender*. She made seventy-one-day round trips carrying containers from the West Coast of the U.S. to the Far East. She then continued via the Panama Canal to the East Coast of the U.S. as far north as New York, and returned to the west coast going as far north as Dutch Harbor, Alaska for frozen fish. Three days were built into the schedule for bad weather. We used all three when fifty-knot winds at Dutch Harbor prevented handling containers. On this run some containers are transshipped to South America at Manzillo Bay on the Atlantic side of the Panama Canal.

Captains and Chief Mates on the largest ships under contract to MM&P, Sea Land and APL containerships, earn about $120,000 a year. To get more ships, the MM&P negotiated special contracts. At the lower end, special contracts permit paying Masters of LASH ships under contract to the U.S. military about $64,000 a year. Very special contracts like sulfur carriers in the Gulf of Mexico, pay Second and Third Mates seventy to eighty dollars a day. I made eighty-five dollars a day as Second Mate in 1974. Retirements annually make room for roughly five to ten new MM&P members. Mates sail in unlicensed capacities to get in line for MM&P membership. When I started sailing in 1967, MM&P had contracts to provide deck officers on nearly all of the approximately 1,200 ships in the U.S. merchant fleet.

Recent MARAD figures reported 265 active, U.S.-flag, oceangoing, self-propelled merchant vessels of 1,000 gross tons and over.

Because jobs are so scarce, owners have the Chief Mate stand a watch, reducing the deck officer complement by one. At Lykes the Chief Mate had the eight A.M. to noon and eight P.M. to midnight watches. Other companies give the Chief Mate a choice of the four to eight or eight to twelve watches. The Lykes Chief Mates did their paperwork on overtime from one to five P.M. The Master, Second, and Third Mates share some duties, but the Chief Mate is still responsible for cargo and ship's maintenance.

Using frozen and precut foods has reduced the number of jobs in the Steward's Department. There are no longer two ABs for deck maintenance. Wipers, the lowest rating in the Engine Department, are gone, as are Electricians. Crew size on old ships dropped from forty-three to thirty six. New U.S.-flag ships have crews of about twenty-one men and women. Some foreign ships carry as few as twelve.

I read that before the Civil War, the U.S. merchant fleet carried eighty percent of U.S. imports and exports. During the Civil War, Union ships were put under foreign flags so that Southern commerce raiders would not destroy them. Owners found the foreign-flag ships cheaper to operate. The amount of U.S. imports and exports carried in U.S. flag ships has never since, with the exception of World Wars I and II and Korea, exceeded forty percent. Currently this amount is a low single digit figure. During shipping recessions, even successful Northern European ship owners, like the Norwegians, transferred their ships to Third World flags and crews, at $5.00 per man per day, to survive. This practice continues as a means of cost saving.

Recent figures place U.S. waterborne foreign trade at 2.7% of the total. In 1960 it was 11.1% and never since exceeded 5.3%.

Captain Wanner:

When United States Lines filed bankruptcy on November 24, 1986, the proceedings in federal court were 352 pages long. One hundred and forty thousand containers of freight from every part of commerce were stranded in every corner of the world. Hundreds of millions of dollars of federally guaranteed ship mortgages were in default.

Captain Sulzer:

Family-run Farrell Lines bought American Export Lines in 1978. Farrell had about thirteen ships in the Africa trades and no experience in India or the Far East, but replaced AEL's agents with Farrell people. Generations of Indian families had been American Export's agents. The new agents did not know the trade, nor did they have the necessary connections to obtain cargoes. I made one more trip to India on the SS Export Buyer. By 1981, Farrell was on its way down to running a few old ships. The liner companies were seeing the end of business as they knew it.

The MM&P threw AEL's Brotherhood of Marine Officers mates off the ships because Farrell had MM&P mates. A strike resulted, and lawsuits were filed. The mates' choice was the MM&P or the Marine Engineers Beneficial Association District I. The majority of us went with MEBA I because, with Farrell losing money at a great rate, ships were sure to be laid up.

In the summer of 1984, several steamship companies told their MM&P officers to join company unions or leave. San Francisco's Tom Crowley, largest tugboat operator in the U.S., had bought Delta Steamship Company of New Orleans for its U.S. Government-subsidized trade routes. He hired me as Chief Mate and sent me to the SS Santa Magdalena in Buenos Aires. Her Captain and Chief Mate had been fired for refusing to join Crowley's union.

The Santa Magdalena was a "combo" built for Grace Line in the mid-1960s, 22,000 tons, 600 feet long, with a capacity of one hundred passengers and 600 containers, with rolling gantry cranes on deck and reefer spaces for bananas. She was fully loaded and being picketed by the International Longshoremen's Association, so there were no line handlers. I went down to the dock and threw off the lines. A large shoreside gangway was in place. I cut its lines with an ax. Due to the pickets, no tugs were available. I dropped the anchor, and the ship turned around it into the stream. Worse still, the fired officers had thrown the charts, stability books, and cargo plan overboard, and the union crew was hostile.

I made two round trips carrying industrial goods from Vancouver, Portland, Seattle, San Francisco, and Los Angeles to Mexico, the east coast of South America, and through the Straits of Magellan to Peru and Columbia. When Mexico's oil credits dried up, we went down empty.

Crowley began tying up ships on their return to the West Coast. I was Captain of the *Santa Magdalena* for one week in 1984, during discharge and lay-up in San Francisco. My next ship was to be a Crowley LASH ship, but he sold them to U.S. Lines. After a coastwise trip on the chemical carrier *SS Keystone Chilbar*, I went back to my Chief Mate's job on New York Maritime's Training Ship Empire State V. When United States Lines went out of business in 1986, Crowley got back three ships, the *SS Sea Wolf*, *Sea Lion*, and *Sea Fox*. He offered me a Master's job. I was working a master's degree in business administration and had married Betty, so I stayed at New York Maritime.

The rise of national fleets, like India, Pakistan, and South Korea, who want the revenue from carrying their own goods, contributes to the decline of the U.S. Merchant Marine. There is a worldwide agreement concerning cargo preference that would give U.S. ships a percentage of the cargoes originating in the U.S. This is the fairest method of allocating cargo among countries. I cannot understand why the U.S. does not participate in this agreement. Bigger ships, each carrying more cargo, mean a smaller number of ships under the U.S. flag. The *SS Export Freedom* carried the cargo of two *Export Aides*. Also, containerized cargoes are collected at fewer places, necessitating fewer port calls and, therefore, fewer ships.

170

Ms. Preston:

Union jobs were drying up by 1978, when I graduated from Kings Point. I wanted steady employment, so I went with Exxon.

Mr. Bullock:

By the late-1980s, uniforms were a thing of the past. Some Captains object to officers looking sloppy on the bridge or in the dining salon. In port we wear company-issued coveralls.

I hold licenses as Second Mate Oceans and Master of 1600-ton vessels. Sailing as Second Mate I sometimes make less than the Third Mate because he or she gets overtime pay for maintaining safety equipment and the hospital and doing reports. The Second Mate's overtime for correcting navigation charts has been cut to two hours per week. In reality, chart corrections could take two hours a day. This cut is dangerous because as a result, many ship don't maintain their charts.

In my union, a mate has to get off a ship after 120 days to make room for another mate. Because jobs are scarce, Captains are earning less than they did as Third Mates and getting half the vacation.

FINISHED WITH ENGINE

Captain Carter:

To reduce chartering costs, Isthmian built a fleet of twenty eight ships between 1920 and 1922. Relatively young Masters and Chief Mates staffed them. Advancement was slow, but I was sailing Chief Mate by January 1937. On arrival in San Francisco, I was instructed to immediately proceed overland to the Marine Superintendent in New York. Ordinarily I enjoyed train travel, but I was apprehensive about what awaited me. He offered me the job of Assistant Pier Superintendent at Isthmian's Baltimore piers, Pier Three Locust Point and Pier One Clinton Street. I held this job for a year or two, working eighty hours a week, usually at night because I was the junior of the two Pier Superintendents.

I married Lena, a Baltimore native. To get away from the long hours on the piers, I became a surveyor for the Board of Underwriters, known since 1955 as the National Cargo Bureau. In 1960, the National Cargo Bureau wanted to promote me to Chief Surveyor in New York City. I looked the job over, even commuted to the office with two of the surveyors. This trip to New York convinced me to stay in Baltimore. I started my own cargo surveying business.

I retired to my summer house on Shipsview Road in Annapolis, Maryland. Ships steam past my picture window going to and from Baltimore on Chesapeake Bay.

Captain Carter departed on his final voyage on August 4, 1990, at age eighty-one.

Commodore Alexanderson:

My wife had cancer. To be with her, I retired from U.S. Lines in 1976. She died in 1979. I married Elizabeth, a widow, in 1983. We all became friends when I came to the Newport News Shipyard years before. Elizabeth's husband made two trips with me on the *United States* before he died.

So I got my wish. I went to United States Lines to get in the passenger ships, and I have no regrets.

> The Commodore and Elizabeth live within the sound of fog horns in Hampton, Virginia.

Captain Atkinson:

To maximize my pension, I made three trips as Second Mate on the *SS Seamar*, a C-4 converted to carry steel from the East Coast and lumber from the West Coast for Calmar Line. On January 6, 1975, I retired from the Masters Mates and Pilots union with thirty-nine years' service.

I was Navigator on the *Freedom*, a one hundred-foot, two-masted schooner, on the Chesapeake Bay from 1975 to 1977. We took her to New York for Operation Sail in 1976.

I got a real estate sales license, but never used it.

About 1980, I was a partner in the *Bloodhound*, a thirty five-foot cabin cruiser out of West Ocean City, Maryland. We did marine archeology on the Maryland coast and wrote articles on the research. The State made us stop.

I'm very involved in the restoration of the Liberty Ship *John W. Brown* in Baltimore.

Looking back, I lived in about the best of times. I was privileged to get a good education in my chosen field before having to face up to the fact of earning a living. Times were tough, work was hard, jobs were few, and wages were low when I started out. I managed to get by without any real hardship, even sent a few dollars home now and then and actually enjoyed my work. Compared to the stories told by the older men of how things were when they started out, we were riding the gravy train.

Captain Atkinson departed on his final voyage on September 25, 1993, at age eighty one.

Captain Fowler:

On the way back from Vietnam on the *SS Oshkosh Victory*, the Chief Engineer repeatedly said that he had enough of the seagoing life and would retire at the end of the voyage. I was also leaning that way. I shouted to the Relief Master as he pulled away from the dock in New York, that I would see him in July. After talking it over with my wife, I retired in 1970, at age sixty, after forty- one years on ships. We moved to a house on Kent Island, Maryland, bought a twenty four-foot cabin cruiser, spent many days fishing and crabbing, and enjoyed life. She passed away in November 1984, one month shy of our fiftieth anniversary.

With my dog, Max, I renovated an old house on an inlet of the Upper Chesapeake Bay in Essex, Maryland. I have an eighteen-foot, open boat and go crabbing or fishing with friends. We have many enjoyable evenings playing pinochle.

I donated my Plath sextant to Project Liberty Ship, an organization restoring the Liberty Ship *John W. Brown* in Baltimore.

Captain White:

Shipping was dead after the Vietnam War. I pensioned out of the MM&P in Baltimore, Maryland in 1970. I then spent six years as Harbor Master of the Gibson Island, Maryland Yacht Squadron. This job gave me experience in smaller yachts, adding to my years in fishing and sailing vessels. I taught a course in celestial navigation to some members of the yacht squadron. Mrs. Henderson, Principal of the Gibson Island School, loaned me a classroom. The turnout on Sunday afternoons amazed me.

For the past several years, I've done yacht brokerage and delivered yachts to the Caribbean. On a delivery from Miami to Singapore, all the way I favorably compared my sights to the positions obtained by the SATNAV. I took command of a native crew of four on a yacht in the Netherlands Antilles. Suzy, a cute Costa Rican utility worker, gave the other crew members VD. I spent more on penicillin than on stores so had to dismiss her, but with a nice letter of recommendation. This experience reinforces my theory that, if you go to sea, you never know what's next. A Chief Mate summed it up for me. As he stumbled into the wheelhouse after falling and skinning his knee in heavy weather, he said, "Damn! What some of us won't do to avoid working!"

With MM&P's authorization, I've accepted delivery assignments, for example, an oilrig from Rhode Island to the North Sea off Scotland.

I was Skipper of an oil-drilling rig in the Red Sea, at the junction of the Gulf of Aqaba and the Gulf of Suez. A British couple on a yacht anchored at Hurghada, Egypt had visited the Gibson Island Yacht Club five years earlier. My signature was in their guest log. I signed it again. Through these retirement jobs I've enjoyed the great diversification in the maritime field.

I spent a few days thinking of retiring to Sailors' Snug Harbor in Sea Level, North Carolina. Then I attended a pool party at the home of my doctor in Pasadena, Maryland. I met his younger sister, Julie, just up from Cuba. She set Snug Harbor back about thirty years. On vacation, we gravitated to south Florida and settled in Surfside. The beach is a five-minute walk from our house. I stay in good physical shape with daily swims in the pool in my yard.

I'm optimistic enough to keep my license and radar endorsement current. The phone rang in 1991. I was asked to take a cargo of tanks to Saudi Arabia for Operation Desert Storm. I couldn't go due to a death in the family.

As I look back on my years, I wouldn't change anything. I always wanted to go to sea. Even if World War II hadn't come, I would have returned to sea. I enjoyed every day of it. However, the U.S. is not a maritime nation. There is no longevity with the companies. Tanker companies especially come and go. But it was interesting work. It isn't money and material things that give happiness in old age. It's rich memories.

Admiral Bauman:

I never could have dreamed when I went to the Federal Building in Boston for my Massachusetts Nautical School interview in 1942, that my office as Rear Admiral commanding the First Coast Guard District would be in the same building, nor that my official residence would be next to the Hospital Point Lighthouse I passed as a "Coal Boat Stiff." As terrible as World War II was, it gave me opportunities I would never have otherwise had.

A painting of the Hospital Point Lighthouse hangs over the mantel in Admiral Bauman's Northern Virginia home.

Captain Schindler:

On February 6, 1984, after 878,702 miles of blue water sailing, I retired to my home near Philadelphia to have time with my wife, daughter, and two sons while they were still young. I'm a marine consultant.

Captain Smeenk:

I got off the *SS Sealand Defender* in time to be home for New year's Eve 1999. My vacation will take me into the spring of 2000, when I'll have thirty years with the MM&P. I'll retire and, under MM&P rules, must leave the maritime industry.

Captain Wanner:

The law said that, after fifteen years in the MM&P Pension Plan, I was one hundred percent vested, so in 1987 I went home to wait for my pension. In 1991, after a lawsuit, I settled my accounts with the union. I spend my time hunting and fishing in Pennsylvania.

GLOSSARY

AB. Able-bodied seaman.

Articles. An agreement between each member of the crew and the Master, stating in what capacity each serves, wages, character and duration of the voyage.

Average. Marine insurance term for a loss.

Beaufort Scale. Indicator of wind speed:

Beaufort Force	State of Air	Wind Velocity in Knots
0	calm	0-1
1	light airs	1-3
2	slight breeze	4-6
3	gentle breeze	7-10
4	moderate breeze	11-16
5	fresh breeze	17-21
6	strong breeze	22-27
7	moderate gale	28-33
8	fresh gale	34-40
9	strong gale	41-47
10	whole gale	48-55
11	storm	56-65
12	hurricane	above 65

Break-bulk. Break-bulk ships carried heavy, bulky cargoes, such as machinery, calling for broken stowage, i.e., space not occupied between and around packages.

Bulwark. Plating forming an extension of a vessel's side above her weather deck.

Bunker. A compartment for stowing coal, which evolved into the term for fuel oil.

Chain locker. A compartment in the forward part of the vessel where the anchor chain is stowed.

Coaming. The portion of a cargo hold extending above the main deck on which the hatch cover is placed.

Conferences. Organizations which sought agreements among member liner companies relative to freight rates, sailing schedules, and ports of call on given trade routes.

Devil's claw. A stopper for the anchor chain, consisting of a turnbuckle, two or three links of chain, and the claw. The claw's two prongs fit over the chain.

Discharge. A certificate given a seaman on completion of a voyage.

Double bottom. The watertight space between a ship's bottom shell-plating and her inner bottom plating.

Down east. A New England destination.

ETA. Estimated time of arrival.

Fathom. Six feet.

Finished with engine (F.W.E.). The log entry that the ship is anchored or made fast to the dock and finished with her engine.

Heave-to. Keep the vessel's head to the wind or sea.

Light. An empty ship.

LORAN. Long Range Aid to Navigation, an electronic navigation system whereby hyperbolic lines of position are determined by measuring the difference in the time of reception of synchronized pulse signals.

Magnitude. The relative brightness of a celestial body.

Ordinary. Ordinary seaman, the entry level position in the Deck Department.

Plimsoll marks. Load line markings painted on the side midships, indicating drafts for fresh and salt water, winter and summer, and certain oceans at which there will still be sufficient reserve buoyancy to insure the safety of the vessel.

Radar. An electronic aid to navigation which determines the distance of an object by measuring the time interval between transmission of a pulse signal and receipt of a signal returned as an echo.

Reefer. Refrigerated cargo space.

Sagging. A vessel is heavily loaded in the middle and lower than both ends.

Slop chest.   Contains clothes, toiletries, and tobacco products for sale to the crew at no more than ten percent above wholesale cost.